For documents to b[...] future ages use **LYONS' INK** It never fades.

THE **BENEDICTINE** OINTMENT

CERTAIN CURE FOR BOILS, CUTS, BURNS, RINGWORM, OLD WOUNDS, SCAB, & EVERY KIND OF SKIN ERUPTION.

SOLE PROPRIETOR
JAMES ANDERSON.
167 Lloyd St
GREENHEYS MANCHESTER.

DAY BOOK   B   COPYING   CASH BOOK   B

THE BOTTLE SEAL

Wm THORNE

VALENTINE'S MEAT-JUICE

TALLY-HO.
BIRKENHEAD.

ISBN 0 9508484 2 5 (Hardback only)

Text set in 7½ pt Helvetica Medium.

ANTIQUE BOTTLES COLLECTORS ENCYCLOPAEDIA

by
Alan Blakeman

Volume 1

Central pictorial motif from an enamel sign for Fremlins Ale. Circa 1920. 3′ x 2′ approx.

BBR Publishing, 5 Ironworks Row, Wath Road, Elsecar, Barnsley, S Yorkshire, S74 8HJ

ACKNOWLEDGEMENTS

Derek Askey
Mick Banks
Eddy Berry
Mike Bithell
Will Van den Bossche
Henry Chesterman
John Clarvis
Laurence Cooper
Mr. & Mrs. Davidson
Steve Day
Peter Douglas
Lembit Eha
John England
Rob Gerhardt
G. & C. Gilbert
Colin Gould
Keith Gretton
Michael Harris
Garry Higgins
Trevor King
Bert Latham
David Lewis
Norman Lewis
Jim Lindeman
Ron Long

Jocelyn Lukins
Bob Macmillan
J. and J. May
Ashley McAvery
Roy Morgan
Hugh Munden
Doctor D. Parry
George Plummer
David Robertson
Mike Sheridan
Keith Shotter
Mike Smith
George Spencer
Barry Stuart
Neville Summers
Brian Thatcher
Doctor Mike Till
David Wastcolt
Nick Waters
Ray Whyborn
Clive & Kae Wicks
Neil Wilcox
Harry Wiley
Mick Wiley
Doctor Anne Young
John Yule

From Collectors on all aspects of collecting covered in these Volumes.

We are particularly interested in photographing collections or receiving black and white photographs of groups of individual items for use in our future volumes.

Also we are interested in purchasing (or obtaining permission to copy) old advertisements related to Collecting in newspapers, magazines, books and trade catalogues etc., in particular:–

e.g. Black and White Magazine
Pharmaceutical Journal
Patents Journal
Chemists and Druggists Diary
Doulton & Watts Co. Ltd.
Bratby and Hinchecliffe
Price & Sons Ltd.
Haywood Tyler Co.
Hardens Star Co.
Kellys Directory of Wines,
   Spirits & Brewing Trades

London Illustrated News
Trade Marks Journal
The Mineral Water Trade Review
Doulton & Co. Ltd.
Codd & Rylands Co.
Maws Son & Thompson Co.
Dairy Supply Co. Ltd.
London Fire Appliances Co.
Warner Ho's Almanac
Burgoyne Burbidge's Cat.
The Pottery Gazette

Any additional information that readers are able to supply for future publications will be greatly appreciated.

Your Obediant Servants,

The 'Ole Bottlemen

5

Cover photographs

FRONT COVER.

Back row;-
1. Amber Harrogate spa bottle £15-£20.
2. Amethyst twisted neck wine (English c1840) £150.
3. Amber Groves & Whitnall codd £20+.
4. Blue top ch. g.b. PONTYPRIDD £120-£150.

Middle row;-
5. Valentines meat extract box & bottle £10+.
6. Beach & Barnicott blue print ointment £7-£10+.
7. James Rowland st. t.t. g.b. £75-£100.
8. Fishers Seaweed Extract £75-£100.
9. English Bellarmine £250-£400.
10. Colourful Doulton made Barnsley Brewery beer jug £600-£800.
11. Sepia Stranraer cream pot £7-£10.

Front row;-
12. Golden amber teakettle £250+.
13. Fortnum & Mason Potted Game pot lid £20+.
14. Large size Submarine poison. £250-£300+.
15. Two dolls heads £10+ each.

BACK COVER;-

Back row;-
1. Circa 1650 shaft and globe wine £1,000+.
2. Large green Hardens Star fire grenade £120-£150+.
3. G Elands, Newcastle cobalt hamilton £150-£200.
4. Silver plated hamilton stand £30-£40.
5. Early labelled Rowats Pickles.

Front row;-
6. Reckitts Blue ceramic pot £40-£50.
7. Miniature Alexandra pot lid & base £150-£200.
8. Ma & Pa Carter inks £80-£100.
9. Miniature t.t. flagon G S Wilson, Alnwick. £30+.

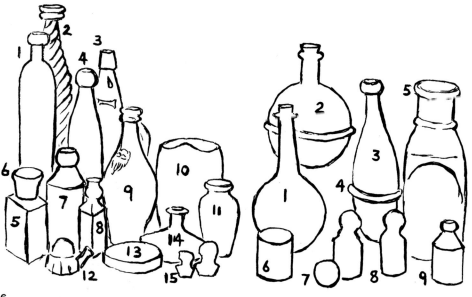

INTRODUCTION

After nearly 20 years of avidly digging, searching and collecting old bottles, jars, pot-lids etc., recovered from our Victorian/Edwardian rubbish dumps, the Hobby is in dire need of a comprehensive range of books. It has built up a sound infra-structure of provincial Bottle Clubs and a full compliment of established regional Bottle Shows together with a specialist quarterly magazine.

Many small booklets, covering narrow specialist fields have served collectors needs quite adequately in the past.

Several price guides have also in their time done valuable service.

Bottle Collecting (BOTTOLOGY) is possibly the most fascinating and pleasurable of the 'new wave' of collecting manias. Discovering our long forgotten rubbish dumps of the Victoria/Edwardian period can bring rewards in more ways than one. Grandma's 'throw-aways' have rapidly become established collectibles/antiques. The actual rubbish of yesteryear has become the antique of to-day!

If you are lucky enough to find an early Victorian tip, the prizes are rich. A whole range of objects d'art are there for the picking. They reveal a fascinating age dedicated to the use of quack medicines, miracle cures, exotic tooth pastes, fragrant creams and delightful designs and colours. Early sealed bottles are another excellent investment but these are not normally dug up. They are usually obtained from cellars, antique shops, junk markets and flea markets.

But locating an early site is not easy. Painstaking research is often needed before grabbing the garden fork and shovel. A browse through old parish and council records or a chat to some of the old locals at the country pub, will often lead to a good site. And when the digging is done, and the spoils cleaned and catalogued, the result can be a tasteful and interesting display.

The antique trade generally remains 'aloof' from trading in old bottles unless they happen to be 17th or 18th century. This becomes very obvious when occasionally a late Victorian bottle such as a coloured dumpy codd bottle is sold in an antique auction and is immediately bid up to three figures by two local enthusiastic bottle collectors (BOTTOLOGISTS). The antique dealers are usually watching with amazement!!

Interestingly enough the majority of bottles collected are well over 80 years old and are considerably older than many items now sold in antique shops.

Bottology has many great advantages over other collecting hobbies – it can be very cheap as all you need is a fork, shovel and a rake (if you are digging dumps) – it can be a family hobby and in many cases is – it provides endless collecting varieties – it can provide an insight into how our Grandparents and Great Grandparents lived – it can also be very educational from an historical point of view for children of all ages – it can help to explain how common household containers were manufactured etc.; etc.

However, our intention here is to encompass the *complete* range of dump dug artifacts, to provide reference listings, category codings, and as accurate a price guide as possible. Eventually the complete set of volumes will form an Encyclopaedic library for the serious collector, hopefully, with a normal price revision list on the lines of the Antique Collectors Club booklets.

The end result to some extent relies upon the assistance and co-operation of the major Clubs and Collectors around the country.

This then is the first Volume. To some it may seem to have a particular bias toward one category, and little, or nothing, on another. All will eventually be included – this first Volume is merely the 'tip of the iceberg'.

A complete and full index for the 1st 2 Volumes will appear at the end of the Volume 2. The indecies for the 'follow-on' Volumes will be at the end of each even numbered volume, e.g. 4, 6 etc.

POSTSCRIPT TO THE SECOND EDITION

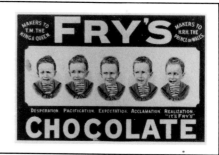

When Gordon Litherland and myself compiled the first edition of the Bottle Encyclopaedia way back in 1986 the Bottle Hobby was already mature with an established range of Shows around the UK, and had just evidenced the very first UK National.

A great deal has changed since then. Tastes and fads have altered considerably. What was once 'hot' might not be so now. Some prices have faltered, some remained stagnant. For the most part shrewd investments have proved extremely wise. All the prices in this second edition have been completely revised and are bang up to date. We have put a price on the old XXX entries too.

Condition remains a prerequisite for investment purposes, although we should not lose sight of the fact that this is after all a hobby - collectors generally acquire items because they like them and not for financial reasons. However, it is reassuring to know the vast majority of good bottles have shown a marked rise in their market value, some quite remarkably so.

The Bottle scene remains much the same - regional Bottle Clubs holding monthly meetings (a few changes as one might expect), some Bottle Shows have disappeared from the calendar only to be replaced by newer ones. Some have floundered some have prospered. The major two-yearly UK National has gone from strength to strength, becoming an important focal point for the hobby with a strong International presence. The content of many Shows has diversified considerably becoming more akin to the American Bottle Fairs. More bric-a-brac, advertising, and later material has crept in. Die hards should not lose sight of the interest potential and nostalgia value of items which were once considered "not old enough!"

Quality items in most every category have continued to dry up, becoming harder and harder to find, resulting in higher values - demand far exceeds supply. With dwindling digging sites this trend is expected to continue.

Codds and patents appear to have struggled during the last few years to maintain their dizzy heights of the mid 1980's. Maybe they rose too sharply and as such are now suffering the penalty? Worldwide collector interest has ensured that the better whisky items, inks and good condition black glass, plus fine pictorial pot lids, have very much led the way. Maybe the strongest rising new 'trend' has been seen in Kitchenalia, although the Pub Jug phenomenon continues strongly, alongside (but seperate in many ways) from the mainstream Bottling fraternity.

BBR has built a reputable Auction service covering most every bottling specialist region. Not only has this proved a bonus to both buyers and sellers but the resulting catalogues, with most every item photographed, condition described, and estimated (followed by the sale results) has armed anyone wishing to with the most up-to-date pricing guides around. The catalogues form very useful reference sources and have provided a stop gap for a general lack of Bottle literature.

An entirely brand new Volume 2 Encyclopaedia within 4 to 6 months of this second edition is planned which will combine to form an unprecedented reference for serious Bottologists.

Suggestions, photographs, and material which you feel would be of use in Volume 2 please do not hesitate to contact the publishers as soon as possible.

bottolergist *n.* ... a person who hath the knowledge of old bottles.

bottology *n.* ... the gathering in of old bottles. (Collecting).

bottologist *n.* ... collector and hoarder of old bottles.

A young digger finds a pot-lid!!

BOTTLE PRICING

We have quoted prices throughout this price guide for "mint" specimens only – that is bottles in "as-new" condition. Chips, cracks, repairs, "smudged" transfers, flaws in manufacture, scratches, stains and sickness however slight – can reduce the price of a bottle significantly.

It must be accepted that some of the rare types of bottle may never be found in a mint condition. In which case it is better to have half a cobalt blue 'sealed shaft and globe' than none at all!!

These volumes provide what they say a 'Price Guide' ultimately the value of any bottle or artefact is what a particular Collector is willing to pay at that time. At the very least you can use our prices on a comparative scale.

Most bottologists at one time only collected items before 1939 when they were still partly hand made (i.e. they had applied lips) but in recent years bottles have been collected right up to the present day. (e.g. milk bottles, ginger beers, commemorative and labelled beers, pub-jugs etc.)

No two bottles are exactly the same and there are a number of factors which can affect the value as listed below.

These factors are also applicable to the other collectibles listed in thse volumes.

Age: Older specimens of the same type usually command higher prices, particularly free-blown types with broken pontils.

Rarity: The fewer examples available the higher the relative price, particularly in one of the popular categories (i.e. Ginger Beers).

Transfer Crudeness: Sometimes bottles take on a crude or dis-figures form during manufacture.

Texture: Variations in the surface of the glass, the number of glass bubbles, stretch marks and changes of colour.

Colour: Unusual, dark, or strong colours or a colour which is rare for that particular bottle.

Embossed or Incised: The clarity of the 'embossing' (the heavier the better), the interest of the actual words or design, the intricacy of the embossing. Ditto for 'incised'.

Dating: The original date of manufacture marked on a bottle. or the indication of the starting date or the use of the particular type of bottle. (i.e. registration number or diamond).

Shape: The aesthetic quality of certain bottles.

Pontil marks: On the base of glass bottles denoting the method and sometimes date of manufacture.

Manufacturer's Mark: These often help with the date of manufacture. Also items are collected all made by one manufacturer. (i.e. Doulton (pottery), Codd & Rylands (glass)).

Mistakes: In the spelling of words or in a design.

Labelled Items: Any item with its original label contents or box will always be of more interest than an 'empty'.

CONTENTS

(Coding letters for different categories shown in brackets)

Code explanation

*The combined volumes of these encyclopaedias will enable collectors to refer to individual items using the code;
e.g. BG7 for a Black Glass Bottle numbered 7 etc. When completed all known types/shapes will be recorded.*

Future Volumes will contain Sections on:–

Blue Glass
Clay Pipes
Commemorative "Dating"-Glass/Pottery
Doll's Head
Fairy Lights
Food
Labelled Bottles
Match Strikers

Milk Bottles
Money Boxes
Mustard Pots
Pickles
Pub-Jugs
Sauces
Soda Syphons
Snuff
Target Balls

Plus extra information on all the Sections in this Volume.

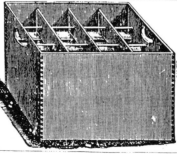

Charles Buckley of New South Wales proudly displays his large "Dewars" "Old Highland Whisky Flagon".

Baby Feeders

The "NURSE MARGERY."

"A TUG OF WAR."

We tend to think of the baby's feeding bottle as a purely 20th century device, and yet 4,000 years ago babies were being treated to the joys of artificial weaning from bottles and feeding cups.

During the Middle Ages mothers who could not breast feed relied upon a cows horn with a scrap of leather acting as a teat. These were replaced by German and Italian wooden or leather feeders, shortly to be upstaged by pewter vessels. However, they harboured germs because they were difficult to clean, this coupled with milk supplies which were often contaminated. Understandably, therefore, hand feeding had a very bad reputation.

The first rubber teat was patented in 1945 in America, previously employing fine cloth, parchment stuffed with sponge, ivory, cork, chamois leather, even cows udder pickled in spirit!

When the baby had cut at least one tooth it was moved onto a 'pap' boat, which aided consumption of a more solid diet – flour or bread boiled in water.

From 1780's up to the late 1880's pottery feeders were used – today the salt glazed and blue and white transferred examples being very highly sought after.

This rare salt glazed feeder was produced to commemorate Queen Victoria's Coronation in 1837. Rarely offered on the open market, expect to pay around £500 - 1,000.

Above: the more remarkable blue and white pictorial feeders are extremely desirable. One sold for £265 at the 1985 Winternational, whilst in complete contrast a bargain was picked up at the 1985 open air Hemel Hempstead Show for £5. In the antiques trade they used to fetch £30 to £100, according to their attractiveness, nowadays they are all a little more 'streetwise!'.

The chances of digging one is rather remote, collectors therefore need to hunt at Bottle Shows, Antique Fayres, Antique Shops, local Auctions, even Car Boot Sales!........£250-£500, Antiques Trade £50-£250+.

Beware of reproductions (much lighter in weight).

Left: The Victorians excelled at ingenious designs and novel inventions, the baby feeder category being no exception. In 1867 Captain Webber patented a design embedding a thermometer in the glass. The Patent Office commented that "such novelties usually take well with the public". 18 years elapsed before S. J. Pocock grasped the idea and marketed the bottle. In 1890 Burroughs Wellcome produced the same basic bottle, which cost 1/3d.   £150-£225.

BABY FEEDERS

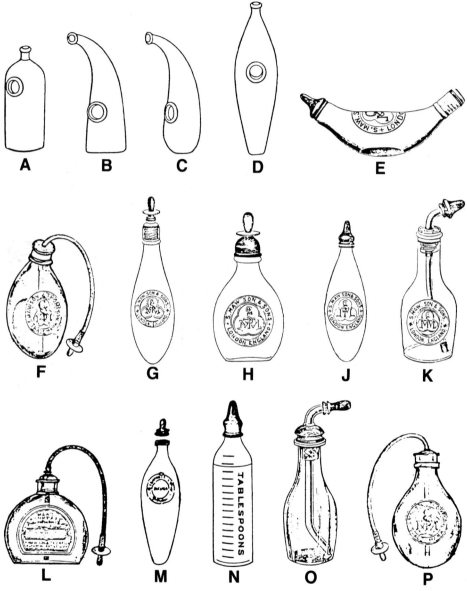

GLASS BOTTLE SHAPES

A. Hand-blown clear glass un-embossed.
B. Hand-blown clear glass un-embossed.
C. Hand-blown clear glass un-embossed.
D. Hand-blown clear glass un-embossed.
E. Aqua embossed with internal screw top.
F. Aqua embossed with internal screw top.
G. Aqua embossed screw top.
H. Aqua embossed with teat-lip.

J. Aqua with pin-hole for air.
K. Aqua embossed with internal screw top.
L. Aqua embossed with tin lip-mount.
M. Aqua embossed with teat-lip.
N. Aqua graduated embossing.
O. Aqua un-embossed with cork top.
P. Aqua embossed with cork top.

Above; Two very unusual free-blown glass shapes. Topmost, type C £75+, whilst below it is a type D £50+ which incorporates a very rare glass teat (this is a German piece).

Glass shapes (see diag. opp.)

A. Hand-blown, clear glass, unembossed........£50+.
B. Hand-blown, clear glass,unembossed..........£75+.
C. Hand-blown, clear glass,unembossed..........£75+.
D. Hand-blown, clear glass,unembossed..........£50+.
E. Aqua, embossed, with internal screw top according to embossing....£5-£10+.
F. Aqua, embossed, with internal screw top, complete with teat, tube and stopper £50-£70, without teat and tube £15+, bottle alone £5-£10.
G. Aqua embossed, screw top...£10-£15.
H. Aqua, embossed, teat-lip, according to embossing...£10-£20.

J. Aqua, with pin hole for air..... £25-£40.
K. Aqua, embossed, with internal screw top, complete with fixtures... £5-£10.
L. Aqua, embossed, with tin-lip mount, according to embossing...£10-£20+.
M. Aqua, embossed , with teat-lip..£5-£10+.
N. Aqua, graduated embossing...£2-£5.
O. Aqua, un-embossed, with cork top..£10+.
P. Aqua embossed, with cork top, according to embossing ...£10-£20.

Pottery shapes, prices can vary alarmingly.

Q. Plain white, sometimes with decorative ribbing..£50-£100+.
R. Blue & White, transferred decoration..£250-£500.
S. Salt glaze stoneware...£500+.

BABY FEEDERS

MAW'S PATENT FEEDING BOTTLES.

1/6
ALEXANDRA FEEDING BOTTLE,
Screw Metal Cap.

2/6
ALEXANDRA FEEDING BOTTLE,
Gilt Porcelain Cap.

1/6
ALEXANDRA FEEDING BOTTLE,
Earthenware Cap.

1/6
ALEXANDRA FEEDING BOTTLE,
Screw Glass Stopper.

1/-
ALEXANDRA FEEDING BOTTLE,
Earthenware Cap.

2/6
FOUNTAIN FEEDING BOTTLE,
Pure Tin Mount.

1/6
FOUNTAIN FEEDING BOTTLE,
Pure Tin Mount.

6d.
ALEXANDRA FEEDING BOTTLE,
Wood-Top Cork.

1/-
OVAL FEEDING BOTTLE,
Earthenware Cap.

1/-
EXPORT FEEDING BOTTLE,
Earthenware Cap.

1/-
EXPORT FEEDING BOTTLE,
Screw Glass Stopper.

1/-
EXPORT FEEDING BOTTLE,
Screw Metal Cap.

6d.
EXPORT FEEDING BOTTLE,
Metal Cap.

6d.
EXPORT FEEDING BOTTLE,
Wood-Top Cork.

6d.
EXPORT FEEDING BOTTLE,
Screw Glass Stopper

6d.
EXPORT FEEDING BOTTLE,
Screw Metal Cap.

Above is a full page advertisement for 16 different variations upon a theme. Note to different stoppers you could select; – wood-top cork, earthenware cap, pure tin mount, screw metal cap, screw glass stopper or a gilt porcelain cap.

Three of the Best
from WESTGATE-ON-SEA

1897 Interesting post card dated 1897 showing three dark green glass-crown top beer bottles. The crown cork was patented in Britain in 1892.

Beers

Glass (corked) bottles were not specifically made to hold beer until the 1870's. From the 17th century beer was put in the same bottles as made for wine and was only sold to the rich in bottles.

The original "porter" bottle was used to hold beer during the period 1780-1840 and was a wine bottle shape usually in black glass with a paper label. (As shown in Advert for Ashby's Pale Ale). These bottles were shipped from English breweries all over the world. (Note: Porter beer was a strong dark beer first brewed in London in 1720).

Glass wine bottle shapes (cylindrical) of the 3-piece and 2-piece mould variety were used from 1820-1870 in a variety of colours.

From 1870 to 1920 heavily embossed bottles were made with lots of interesting details such as the name of the brewery, the address, pictorial trade marks etc. it is these bottles that are the most popular with collectors.

During this period there was also the introduction of a variety of closures apart from the cork. i.e. Internal screw stopper, swing stopper, crown cork etc. (Described in the Mineral Waters Section).

After this period up until the present day most beers are collected for their interesting labels (commemorative etc.) or their rarity.

Stoneware wine bottles (corked), were also used to hold beer from the 17th century to the early part of the 18th century, when stoneware bottles were specifically made to contain beer but not in great quantities. The glass 'porter' shaped bottle was copied in stoneware and even some of the other cylindrical types have the word 'porter' incised in them.

Later transfer printed beers were used mainly for no-alcoholic types. (1870-1930).

ASHBY'S AUSTRALIAN PALE ALE.

THIS ALE, which has for many years been shipped to the Australian markets, where it is in high repute, resembles in those properties for which it is so strongly recommended by the faculty, the East India Pale Ales; but being brewed for a climate of lower temperature, and possessing a finer flavour and greater body, it will be found more congenial to the British taste. The attention of families is especially invited to this Ale, as it is particularly adapted to private use. It may be had, and bottled in excellent condition, in casks of 9 and 18 gallons, as received from the Brewery, at Staines; of Wm. Hancock, 83, Connaught-terrace, London Agent. Orders by post (free) punctually attended to.

This advertisement appeared in a Newspaper in 1840.

Cork-top, embossed, aqua ....£1-£2.
Cork-top, embossed, green......................£2-£2+.
Cork-top, embossed, brown.....................£1-£2+.
Cork-top, embossed, amber.....................£1-£2.
Cork-top, embossed, black......................£2-£20+.
Screw-top, embossed aqua.....................£1-£2.
Screw-top, embossed, green...................£1-£2+.
Screw-top, embossed, brown..................£1-£2+.
Screw-top, embossed, amber..................£2-£5+.
Screw-top, embossed, black..................£2-£5+.
Crown-top, embossed, aqua....................£1-£2.
Crown-top, embossed, green...................£1-£2.
Crown-top, embossed, brown...................£1-£2.
Crown-top, embossed, amber...................£1-£2.

Cork-top, embossed, dumpy, green...........£2-£5.
Cork-top, embossed, dumpy, brown ....£2-£5.
Cork-top, embossed, dumpy, black.........£3-£10+.
Miniature, embossed, less than 4"............£15+.
Display, embossed or labelled, over 2'........£50+.
King's Ale, label, full, 1 pint...........................£30.
King's Ale, label, full, 1 quart.........................£30.
King's Ale, label, empty, 1 pint......................£15.
King's Ale, label, empty, 1 quart...................£30.
Prince's Ale, label, full, 1 pint.......................£20.
Prince's Ale, label, full, 1 quart....................£30.
Prince's Ale, label, empty, 1 pint..................£10.
Prince's Ale, label, empty, 1 quart................£20.

Group of labelled beers, left to right: 1 pint, King's Ale, full (1902) - £30; 1 pint, Prince's Ale, (1929) - £20; 1/2 pint, Bass & Co's Pale Ale, black-£15; 1 pint, Prestonpans Beer, black- £15.

A selection of card, enamel, tin & paper advertising, respectively;
1. Multi-coloured 'Ind Coope & Cos' card ad showing 3 of their range of Ales. 26" x 20". £100+.
2. Superb, almost full figure size, multi-coloured beer-label-shaped enamel for Godsall & Sons, Ales & Stouts. £350-£400+. 3. Small pressed tin sign, circa 1920's, for Blackburn Brewery showing fine detailed motor dray. £250-£300+. 4. Small paper ad for 'Gilmours Oatmeal Stout', between the wars. £25-£50.

BITTERS

In England, during the reign of George II, the government, in an effort to control the wholesale drunkenness of the working class, levied a heavy tax upon gin, which was the then cheap spirit consumed in vast quantities.

Not to be denied a lucrative market, liquor manufacturers steeped a few harsh tasting herbs in gin and called the concoction "bitters" (or "gripe" or "colick water").

However, myth, and faith, arose over the medicinal value of such mixtures, and much deceptive advertising, the bane of the medicine man, plagued the trade.

The 'bitters' differed between the U.K. and U.S., their prohibition laws created a giant upsurge in the sales of bitters. Today it is their No. 1 collecting category? Here, though, it remains relatively untapped, but the range is certainly far greater than we can imagine, especially if we witness the records in the trade journals of the Victorian period.

KHOOSH
The King of Bitters

A	WITH
	SHERRY,
FINE	GIN, OR
APPETISER	WHISKY

THE CHEMISTS' AND DRUGGISTS' DIARY, 1912

23

DR. SOULE'S
HOP BITTERS.

THE ONLY SPRING AND SUMMER MEDICINE which has stood the test of time for fifty years. It is famous by reason of its many virtues. If you are WEAK AND LOW-SPIRITED, TRY IT. If you are in the Workshop or on the Farm, in fact, anywhere, and you feel that your System needs cleansing, toning, and stimulating, TAKE IT. If you ARE A MAN OF BUSINESS, weakened by the strain of your duties, avoid stimulants, and you will have new life and vigour if you insist upon having a course of

DR. SOULE'S HOP BITTERS.

If you want BALMY SLEEP, GOOD DIGESTION, RICH BLOOD, PERFECT HEALTH, have always by you Dr. Soule's Hop Bitters. Young or old, rich or poor, if your blood is impoverished, pulse feeble, nerves unsteady, and faculties dull, don't physic and physic, for it weakens and destroys, but take a few doses of

DR. SOULE'S HOP BITTERS.

The Invalid Wife, Mother, Sister, or Child can be made the Picture of Health, and, remember, you will be restored to Health and Beauty, for neither ill-health nor disease can possibly exist against a course of

DR. SOULE'S HOP BITTERS.

ONE DOSE LAST THING AT NIGHT GIVES A NIGHT'S REPOSE.

It is not a vile concoction, pretending to be made of wonderful foreign roots, barks, &c., and puffed up by long bogus certificates of miraculous cures, but a simple, pure, effective medicine made of well-known valuable remedies, and furnishes its own certificates by its cures.

One Bottle contains more real HOP STRENGTH than a Barrel of ordinary Beer.

To all whose employments cause IRREGULARITY of THE BOWELS or urinary organs, or who require an appetiser, tonic, and mild stimulant, this medicine is invaluable, being highly curative, tonic, and stimulating, WITHOUT INTOXICATING. Sold by all chemists and medicine vendors. Be sure and see the Green Hop Cluster is on the label. Ask for Dr. Soule's; none other is genuine. If you cannot get Dr. Soule's, write to THE HOP BITTERS COMPANY, 41, Farringdon Road, London.

In America Asa Soule used his own name to promote the sales of his hop bitters in the U.K., whilst in the States his 'medicine' was called Dr. Doyles!

Embossed on four neck panels it reads 'Dr. Soules Hop Bitters, 1872' with a hop plant embossed on the front panel.

The advertisement above strongly lays claim to its many curative powers.

Surprising how better you feel when tipsy or drunk?

Right; A superbly embossed green beer-bottle-shape which comes in quart and pint capacities. Both feature the bust of the English Naval Commander Rodney.

1. 'Blackshaws Hop Bitters, Stourport'. Aqua dumpy beer bottle shape, with blob top. Very rare. £5-£10+.
2. 'Gwilym Evans, Quinine Bitters'. Aqua, panelled, medicine shape, S. Wales. £2-£5.
3. 'Helibrons Aromatic Bitters', tall aqua bottle with ladies leg neck. Ex. Rare. £30+.
4. Khoosh Bitters, large brown bottle with raised rings on neck and 2 down the sides. £15-£20.
5. Knight & Co., Hop Bitters, Pontycymmer. T.t. g.b. type. £7-£10+.
6. Soules Hop Bitters, large size. Amber/brown. £15-£20.

7. As previous but 1/2 size, much rarer. £30-£50.
8. Taylors Hop Bitters. St. g.b. shape, black transfer shows jockey riding a beer bottle. £75-£100.
9. Taylors Hop Bitters, large quart green, beer bottle shape. Pictorial t.m. of Admiral Rodney in centre. £10-£15.
10. As previous but one pint size. £5-£10.
11. Wheatleys Hop Bitters, Bristol. Dense black glass beer bottle shape, embossed with beacon t.m. Very rare. £8-£10+.

Above; L. to R; type 8, Taylors Hop Bitters with jockey on bottle, amber Dr. Soules Hop Bitters, type 7, and a t.t. g.b. shape 'Knight & Co. Hop Bitters, Pontycymmer', S. Wales, type 5.

A – BLOW PIPE.   B – LITTLE WINDOW.   C – MARBLE.   D – FORCEPS.   E – MOULDS BY MEANS OF WHICH THE SHAPES ARE PRODUCED.
Early 18th century glass house, from a wood-cut of the period. Note the broken onion bottle in the foreground.

Black Glass

Black glass in terms of bottle collecting refers to glass bottles that look black because of the reflection of light from them. Usually the actual colour is usually dark brown/amber or olive/green which can be seen when the bottle is held up against the light, particularly with the free-blown types where the walls of the bottle are sometimes very thin.

Also usually included in this category are darker amber/brown and olive/green glass bottles that don't actually look black. There is a wide variety of black glass bottles in all shapes and sizes.

From the earliest free-blown shaft and globe wine bottles to the late Victorian heavily moulded beer bottles. This means that you can pay £1 for a beer bottle or several thousand pounds for dated early shaft and globe sealed wine bottle!

We have illustrated the evolution of the shape of the wine bottle. There are also more unusual shapes for each period and these are always rarities. (i.e. Square onion, wide-mouth onion, octagonal bottles etc.)

Moulded bottles are also very attractive and come in all shapes and sizes usually with broken pontil marks on the base up until 1860. The most popular are the ones with interesting embossed lettering and trade marks etc.

In this section free-blown bottles are included which date from approx. 1600 to 1820. From 1820 to 1860 most bottles were moulded, but free-blown bottles were made of the "Nailsea" and "Alloa" type, during this period.

"Jackson and Company Distillers - Dockhead London'. Black glass whisky flask found in two sizes 6 ins. and 9 ins. £100-£200, (c. 1830-1850).

Small size black glass "Daffy's Elixir" with broken pontilled base (extremely rare) - £500-£750+, (c.1820-1830).

Opposite page; Black glass bottle shapes

1. "Sealed" shaft and globe (c.1660-70). £2,000-£5,000+.
2.. The first onion shaped bottle (c.1680-90). £200-£300.
3. An early "sealed" shaft and globe (c.1650-60). £3,000-£7,000+.
4. A European case bottle (c.1780-1820). £30-£50+.
(These bottles are sometimes found in mahogany cases in sets of 3 with paper labels: "Brandy", "Gin" and "Whisky").
5. Free-blown Dutch case gin bottle (c.1760-1800). £30-£50+.
6. Typical free-blown sealed wine bottle (c.1780-1800). £30-£70 (dated £100+).
7. Extremely rare "sealed" black and white "Nailsea" flask (dated 1809). £500-£700+.
8. Squat wine bottle showing transitional shape from the mallet to the cylindrical wine bottle. (c. 1760). *Drawing by Brian Johnson.* £40-£50.

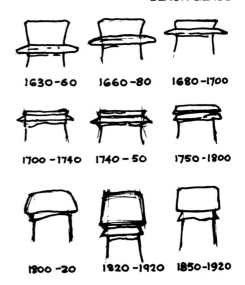

1630-60   1660-80   1680-1700

1700-1740   1740-50   1750-1800

1800-20   1820-1920   1850-1920

Development of the string rim and bottle lip on English wine bottles.

Wine bottle shapes showing the transition from the 'mallet' to the 'cylinder'. (1730-1770).

29

A very attractive varied group of free-blown (dip-moulded), broken pontilled based, wide mouth black glass bottles, vividly showing the crudeness to be found in hand-made glass. (c.1780-1850). £50-£100+.

Black glass embossed master ink - 'Todd's Perth Ink' (There are 2 versions of this bottle this is the earlier one. The later one has no serifs on the lettering)-£30-£50.

Two black glass octagonal, dip-moulded, broken pontilled based, wines or chemists bottles (c. 1800-1840)-£250-£400+.

Three black glass contrasting beers from the North East. This photograph illustrates the attraction of collecting black glass beers - some to be found with impressive pictorial trade marks. L. to R. "Vaux & Sons" - "Sunderland" - £5; "W. H. Wood" - "Durham" - £8; "William Rowe, Newcastle-on-Tyne" - £5.

Rare crude black glass embossed octagonal beer "F. LYON, ECCLESTON" (c.1870) - £30-£40.

Two black glass large chemists free-blown, broken pontilled based, with gilt labels (c.1800-1840) - £75-£100+.

Magnificent black glass "Nailsea" type serving bottle (c 1840) (Scottish) - £300+.

THE "HOOPED" PAN.
(Round)
Very striking and bold.

In three styles—Maroon and Gold, Blue and Gold, or Green and Gold, with "New Milk" in gold letters.

	£	s.	d.
Capacity—12 quarts ..	4	6	6
„ 18 „ ..	6	0	0

THE "ROSEBUD" PAN.
(Round)
White ground, decorated with flowers in colours, shaded pale blue decoration. "New Milk" in gold letters.

	£	s.	d.
Capacity—12 quarts ..	3	0	0
„ 18 „ ..	3	15	0

THE "MEADOW" PAN.
(Round)
Well executed Farm View in Colours.

	£	s.	d.
Capacity—12 quarts ..			
„ 18 „ ..			

THE "MAYFAIR" PAN.
(Oval)
Very handsome design.

The best class pan that is made. In various colours—Yellow, Pink, Maroon, Light Green, Dark Green, and Salmon, freely decorated in Gold, "New Milk" in gold letters and festoons of wild flowers in natural colours.

	£	s.	d.
Capacity—18 quarts ..	8	0	0

THE "ALBION" PAN.
(Round)
A cheap and attractive pan.

In Pure White with "New Milk" in plain bold black letters.

	£	s.	d.
Capacity—12 quarts ..	1	7	6
„ 18 „ ..	2	2	0

THE "FARM" PAN.
(Round)
With floral decoration and farm scene, green grass, cows in black.

	£	s.	d.
Capacity—12 quarts ..	3	5	0
„ 18 „ ..	4	18	6

Taken from Catalogue dated 1923: Dairy Supply Co., London.

Butter Crocks

DAIRY SUPPLY CO., LTD., MUSEUM ST., LONDON, W.C.1.

DAIRY SUPPLY CO., LTD., MUSEUM ST., LONDON, W.C.1.

When the first few Maypole Dairy & Buttercup Dairy crocks appeared, now more than a decade ago, they received a relatively luke-warm reception. Maybe it was because they did not fit any of the established collecting categories, certainly cream pot collectors were somewhat uncertain. Fashions and taste have changed considerably, and now there are a large number of different butter crocks recorded. Even cream pot collectors view them more favourably, along with the Kitchenalia brigade and general bottle collectors. The peripheral 'Habitat' set use them to store eggs, upon their trendy pine Welsh dressers. The better pictorials even rank alongside whisky jugs for the impact, and detail, of their transfers.

1. Buttercup Dairy Co., cow facing R., 7lb size. Buchan made. £50-£75.
2. Danish Dairy Co., two tone, 7lb., shapely milk maid. £200+.
3. Wm. Frame & Sons, Family Grocer, Glasgow. Large cow facing L. £300-£400.
4. General Supply Assoc., two tone, blue print, non pictorial. £50+.
5. Maypole Dairy Co. Ltd. two tone, maypole pictorial. 1lb size. £50-£70.
6. As previous, but 2lb size. £50+.
7. As previous two, but 3lb size. £50+.
8. A. P. Suttie, two tone, impressed wording picked out in blue. £40+.

One of 1984's best butter/cream related finds was this 'Wm Frame & Sons, Family Grocers, Glasgow' butter crock. Type 3, surely worthy of a £300-£400 price tag now? This example is extra wide compared to the more normal crocks.

BUTTER CROCKS

Above; three different sizes of butter crocks. L. to R., type 8 £40+, centre , type 6, 2lb capacity, £50+. R. 7lb size Buttercup Dairy Co., type 1 £50-£75. Exactly the same transfer is often printed upon the different sized crocks, collectors generally prefer the smaller sizes with a fuller fitting transfer!

Above; delightful Danish Dairy Co., with pretty, shapely, milk maid. The two tone rim is always a runny brown type. This, type 2, is valued at £200+.

CAVIARE POTS

Caviare has always been the delight of the rich, the roe of the sturgeon being a relatively scarce commodity. Maybe because it was such an expense the pots were made especially sturdy, often of a very thick pottery manufacture, maybe so designed to help keep the contents cool? Whatever the real reasons they have, as a result, survived remarkably well in bottle dumps – rarely are they discovered broken.

However, caviare pots are still a relatively neglected field, though general 'Kitchenalia' collectors (just one of the many mainstream offshoots from this hobby?) have aided an upward trend in some of the prices.

Left to right; types 3, 11, 9, 1, 6 & 8.

1. **Fresh Caviare**, 3 3/4 ins. tall, t.t., barrel shape £5-£10.
2. **Fortnum & Mason Ltd.**, 182 & 183 Piccadily, W. Several sizes. Pot lid with transfer of sturgeon on the base-side. £20-£30.
3. **Rt. Jackson & Co. Ltd.**, 3 1/4 ins. tall. Marked Doulton, Lambeth. Transfer on front and back. £10-£15.
4. **John Miller**, Finsbury Pavement, E.C. (London?), 3 3/4 ins., impressed salt glaze, very bulbous body shape. CX patent on reverse. £5-£10.
5. **H. Monoroff**, the Astrachan Caviare Co., 4 3/4 ins. tall, tubular pot. £50-£70+.
6. **Morel Bros.**, Cobbet & Son Ltd., 18 & 19 Pali Mall, London, S.W. 3 3/4 ins., impressed salt glaze, very bulbous body shape. CX patent on reverse. £10-£15+.

7. **Morel Brothers**, 210 & 211 Piccadilly, 4 1/2 ins. tall, impressed. Two tone salt glaze. Patent HH on reverse. £5-£10.
8. **The Russian Caviare Co.**, 3 1/4 ins. tall, underglaze transfer. £10+.
9. **Selfridge's** Delicatessen Dept., 2 1/4 ins. tall, with lid. Skey, Tamworth pottery mark on base. £5-£10.
10. **Sweeting & Co.**, Cheapside. 3 1/4 ins. tall, impressed, t.t. £5-£10.
11. **Wm. Tong & Sons**, 4 1/2 ins. tall. Impressed 'Fresh unpressed Astrachan Caviare imported by Wm. Tong & Sons, 20, 21 and 22 Scale Lane, Hull. Doulton & Watts pottery mark. £20-£30+.
12. **G. Zalinoff**, 3 1/4 ins. tall, transferred. £10-£15.

CAVIARE POTS

Above left; types no. 2, two different Fortnum & Masons pot lids with the all-important bases featuring the pictorial of the sturgeon itself. £20-£30 and rising due to the considerable interest in 'Kitchenalia.'. Right type 12; the 'G. Zallinoff' transferred pot. £10-£15.

Above; four shapes displaying the variety of styles available. Left type 8; 'The Russian Caviare Co., Russian & Continental Stores, 10 James Street, Haymarket, S1, by appointment' and featuring a detailed coat of arms. £10+. Centre type 5; the £50-£70+ value on this Monoroff cylinder belies its actual rarity. Right type 7 & 10; Morel Bros. and Sweetings salt glazed examples. £5-£10.

CREAM
JUGS.

It was Chris Hunt who firmly established this facet of the hobby. He laid the foundations with two thoroughly compiled books, now sadly out of print. From this comprehensive platform eager cream pot collectors chase their beloved little pots, ever on the look out for new discoveries, and the colourful tops, transfers, or the very special pictorials.

During the last couple of years the rarest and best examples have risen dramatically in price. Demand for these far exceeds supply.

This is not difficult to understand why, for they take up little space yet display beautifully. Even the commoner types look impressive, especially in a modern kitchen setting.

Looking back in history it was a number of factors which led to the increased popularity in the use of pottery cream jugs; the expanding railway system, wider use of refrigeration, and the mechanical cream separator. From the 1880's the market escalated, even though the commodities' expense remained a limiting factor.

After the First World War the increasing cost of both labour and materials saw their demise, in favour of waxed paper cups.

Today it is the transferred examples, especially the pictorials, which capture the imagination and hearts (and often wallets?) of the dedicated collector. Evocative and enchanting farm scenes, peaceful cows in England's green and pleasant land, all combine to make them as irresistible now as their past contents.

THE " CREAM " JUG.
Decorated in various styles.
Capacity, about 1 quart .. **11/0**
    ,,   about 2 quarts .. **14/-**

The black transferred Wigtownshire Creamery Co., Stranraer. One of the commonest pictorial jugs available, around £3-£5. However, this photo reveals the charm and detail available which make cream pots so very popular. The sepia version, type 38 at £7-£10 or more, has to be a contender for one of the best value-for-money bottles available, particularly when the transfer is crisp.

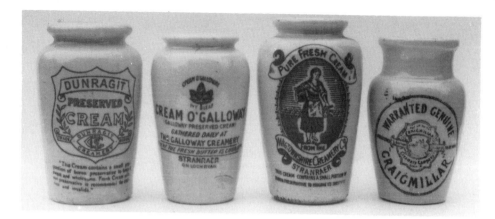

Above; four quite common pots, L. to R.; type 13 £3-£5, type 18 £3-£5, type 38 (sepia) £7-£10, type 8 £3-£5..

Cream pots can be displayed easily, in a relatively small area. This Show display also incorporated a few dairy-related items of ephemera – post cards, trade cards etc.

1. **Annandale Dairy Co.**, Dundee & Lockerbie, black print of cow, 3 1/2 ins. £20-£25.
2. **A. Davy,** black print, lip and handle, squat shape 3 ins. £15+.
3. **Bolesworth's Prize Dairy,** horse & cart pictorial, black print, green top, 5 ins. £300+.
4. **Belgravia Dairy Co. Ltd.,** churn with handle, green print, Belleek pottery, 3 1/2 ins. £75+.
5. **Buttercup,** milkmaid and cows head, blue top and blue transfer, 4 1/2 ins. & 5 ins. £30-£35+.
6. **J. E. Bannister,** Huddersfield, milkmaid in field of cows, brown top, lip and handle, 4 ins. & 5 ins. £20+.
7. **Boams,** Ardwick, Manchester, blue print, 3 ins. & 3 3/4 ins. £3-£5.
8. **Craigmillar,** black print, 4 1/2 ins. £3-£5.
9. **C.W.S. Ltd.,** Brislinton, Somerset, brown top churn, 3 3/4 ins. £25-£30+.
10. **Crystal Brook Band,** man and 3 cows pict., green top and green print, 4 ins. £50-£75+.
11. **Dalbeattie Creamery,** milkmaid and cow, black print, red/brown top, 4 1/2 ins. £20-£30.
12. **Derbyshire Dairies,** Leeds, cows head pict., all white, pouring lip. £50+.
13. **Dunragit Creamery,** Preserved Pure Cream, black print, 4 1/4 ins. £3-£5.
14. **Duneane Creamery,** Ronaldstown, Co. Antrim, cow, milkmaid, black print, 4 1/2 ins. £25-30.
15. **Express Dairy Co. Ltd.,** dairy show 1888, blue top, blue print, 4 ins. £40-£50+.
16. **Excelsior Dairy Co.,** Normanby by Spital, Lincoln, brown top, handle, 4 ins. £10-£15.
17. **Golden pastures,** thick rich cream, cow and milkmaid pictorial, blue top & print, 4 ins. £25-£30.
18. **Galloway Creamery,** black print of maple leaf, 4 1/4 ins. £3-£5.

19. **Greenwoods,** Harpurhey Creamery, Manchester, 3 ins. £3+.
20. **Hailwood's Jubilee,** lip and handle, Q. Victoria portrait, black print, 4 ins. £150-£200.
21. **Hailwood's Rich Cream,** black print of cow, brown top, 3 ins. & 3 1/2ins. £3+.
22. **Hammersley's Creamery,** Broughton, blue/black print, 3 ins., 3 1/2 ins. & 4 1.2 ins. £3+.
23. **Helsby Creamery,** red-brown topped churn, 3 3/4 ins. £15-£20.
24. **Horner's Devonshire Clotted Cream,** red print tube shape, 4 1/2 ins. £20-£30.

25. **Ideal Dairy Co.,** 222 Kendal Road, London, brown top and print, 3 ins. £10-£15.
26. **Imperial Creamery,** Glasgow, black print of milk churn, green top, 4 1/2 ins. £200-£250.
27. **Jordan & Pawley,** Primrose Dairy, 16 King Street, Maidstone, green top, 3 ins. £30-£40.
28. **Jersey Cream,** Sandygate, all white, black print of cow, 3 ins. £10-£15.
29. **Lancashire Hygienic Dairies,** brown top, black print, 3 ins. & 4 ins. £3+.

CLOTTED CREAM POTS.

White Earthenware

Quarter-pound,		
	4/-	per dozen.
		per gross.
Half-pound,		
	5/9	per dozen.
		per gross.

Though the cylindrical cream pot is, in general, a scarce shape, a large number of different ones are now recorded. They also include an impressive range of transfer colours; sepia, brown, red, purple, blue, green. The advertisement reveals the trade cost of the jugs in quarter pound and half pound capacities – 4d to 6d each .... and that without the contents?

30. **Nidderdale Creameries,** Harrogate, black print of cow, lip & handle, 3 ins & 4 ins. £7-£10.
31. **Provincial Dairies,** Ilkley, black print of cow & calf rocks, lip, 4 ins. £50-£70.
32. **Parrott & Axe Vales,** Crewkerne, Som., black print of factory, 4 1/4 ins. £8-£10.
33. **Rose Bower Dairy Co.,** Abbey Pasture, black print of Abbey, 3 1/2 ins. £80-£120.
34. **Strathbogie Dairy,** milkmaid and cow, blue print, 4 3/4 ins. £8-£12.
35. **Urney Creamery Ltd.,** Co. Tyrone, blue top, blue transfer, 4 1/2 ins. £75-£100.
36. **Webster's Fresh Dairy Cream,** Halifax & Hipperholme, lip & handle, 3 3/4 ins. £7-£10.
37. **Williams & Co.,** Crouch End Creamery, blue top, blue cow pict., 4 ins. £50-£60.
38. **Wigtownshire Creamery Co.,** Stranraer, sepia print of milkmaid, 4 ins. £7-£10.

Right; One of the most dramatic cream jug transfers, and the only dated pot, so far (?) is this '1881 First Prize' cylinder dug up in 1984. Though badly cracked it remains the only example so far recorded and rates very highly indeed. For a mint one a sure case for price by negotiation, or a sound auction lot!

Above; a display of cylinders showing the two sizes made, though that far left is fatter, and therefore not quite as high.

Quack Cures

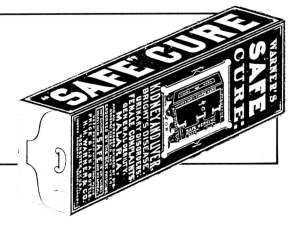

Quack cures, though not yet as keenly collected an area as in America (where it is one of their most popular categories), continues to win new devotees by virtue of both the wild claims often made of the past medicines, as well as appealing to the glass collector by virtue of the variety of shapes and colours found.

Alan McEwens first book laid the foundations, and his eagerly awaited follow-up should further boost the category, in an area where personal library research can often be so rewarding! Most prices have remained stable, though the rarities show expected upward movement. Still an area, though, where the new collector can do remarkably well.

A magnificent array of coloured medicines and quack cures. All of the back row are products from George Handysides, whilst mixed amongst the rest are Warners, Prices, a coloured Daffys, Fishers Seaweed Extract etc.

QUACK CURES

Above; a very fine range of black glass Handysides bottles, produced for the poverty stricken mining areas of the North East of England, where illness and disease were commonplace at the time. L. to R. type 29, a small sized Blood Purifier, type 28, type 24, an aqua version of type 29 (very rare), and another small Blood Purifier in green glass.

1. **Alicsalutice,** the cure for all rheumatic pain. 5 3/4 ins. tall, aqua. £15+.

2. **Alicsalutice,** the cure for all rheumatic pain. 5 3/4 ins. tall, amber. £50+.

3. **Bells** certain cough cure, 6 ins., aqua. £3.

4. **Bennetts 'Hyssop'** cure, Stockport. 5 1/4 ins., aqua-green. £5-£10.

5. **Billingtons** cough cure, Barnsley. 4 1/2 ins., aqua. £7-£10.

6. **Bishops** granular citrate of caffeine, headaches cured. 6 ins. copper blue. £3-£5.

7. **Bronkura.** 6 ins., deep aqua. £7-£10.

8. **Dr. Browns** cough cure. (Kent?) 5 1/4 ins., aqua. £5.

9. **Bronko** cures coughs, colds, bronchitis etc. Ice blue. £7-£10.

10. **Curechilene** .. cures cattle diseases. 7 1/2 ins., aqua. £2-£3.

11. **Calverts Derby** cure for colds and influenza. 5 1/4 ins. Aqua. £5-£10.

12. **Cherokee** kidney & liver cure, London, Seven Barks. 5 1/4 ins., aqua. £30+.

13. **'Chairmender'** ... cures ... thowd cheer bottomer. (Bury) 5 ins., aqua. £15-£20+.

14. **Cundalls** wild cherry pictoral ... cure. 5 ins., aqua-green. £7-£10.

15. **Daffys Elixir,** non pontilled, aqua. £25-£30.

16. **Dalbys** Carminative, non pontilled type £15+.

17. **Days** cough cure. 5 1/4 ins., aqua. £5-£10.

18. **Eatons** fruit cough cure. (London). 5 ins., aqua. £7-£10.

19. **Elepizone** a safe cure for fits & epilepsy, London. 7 1/2 ins., pale blue. £1-£2:

20. **Fennings** Fever Curer. 6 3/4 ins., aqua. £1-£2.

21. **Fishers** seaweed extract, Ulverston. Unique bright green triangular shaped bottled with bulb neck £70-£100+.

22. **Fords** balsom of horehound. Rectangular base, pontilled, aqua. £40-£50+.

Above; Warners are collected the world over by keen quack cure collectors. The six shown give the range of sizes available.

23. **Hagues** kura-a-kof, Lincoln. Aqua. £5+.
24. **Handysides** blood food, medicine bottle shape. 5 1/4 ins., black. £15-£20.
25. **Handysides** blood food, medicine bottle shape. 10 3/4 ins., green. £20+.
26. **Handysides** blood purifier, panelled, square body, long neck. 10 3/4 ins., black. £70+.
27. **Handysides** consumption cure, sauce bottle shape. 6 1/2 ins., green. £25-30+.
28. **Handysides** consumption cure, sauce bottle shape, black - up to 8 ins. £25-£30+.
29. **Handysides** consumption cure, gin shape, octagonal neck. 11 ins., black. £100-£120.

30. **Handysides** drink preparation, square. 10 3/4 ins., green. £30-£50.
31. **Handysides** easily digested syrup. 6 ins., green. £50-£70.
32. **Hartleys** cough cure. 5 ins., aqua. £5.
33. **Holdens** Tommy bottle, chicken on nest pictorial. 4 1/2 ins., aqua-blue. £15-£20+.
34. **Dr. Hairs** asthma cure, London. 6 ins., aqua. £5+.
35. **Dr. Hairs** asthma cure, London. 6 ins., amber. £7-£10.
36. **Jacksons** antizyme or fever cure, Bawtry. Aqua. £7-£10.
37. **Dr. Kilmers** swamp root, kidney, liver & bladder cure. Sample, 3 1/4 ins., aqua £2+.

QUACK CURES

Opposite; original advertisement featuring a labelled bottle of Prices Glycerine, embossed on rear 'Prices Patent Candle Co.' with actual labelled bottle alongside. Both are word for word the same. This type 48 wedge shaped cure commands £60-£75, surely because of its stunning cobalt colour. Only a handful are recorded with labels intact. One amber example seen years ago - whereabouts now unknown!

38. **Dr. Kilmers** swamp root, kidney, liver & bladder cure. Sample, 4 1/4 ins., aqua. £2-£3.

39. **Dr. Kilmers** swamp root, kidney etc., etc. Embossed lungs. 8 ins., aqua £30+.

40. **Dr. Lanes** catarrh cure. 6 3/4 ins., aqua. £7-£10.

41. **Lesters** cough cure. (Warwickshire chemist), aqua. £8-£10.

42. **Liqufruta** cough cure. 5 1/4 ins., aqua-green £3-£5.

43. **Dr. Mackenzies** smelling bottle catarrh cure, with stopper. 2 1/2 ins., olive-green. £7-£10.

44. **Extract of mistletoe** the druid cure. Celtic priest pictorial. Definitely a myth?

45. **The Manchester** cough cure. 4 3/4 ins., aqua-green. £7-£10.

46. **Pisos** cure for consumption. 5 ins., aqua £1-£2.

47. **Pisos** cure for consumption. 5 ins., olive-green. £5-£7.

48. **Prices patent Candle Co.**, wedge shape with diamond reg. Cobalt. £60-£75.

49. **Radams** microbe killer, man striking skeleton. English version 10 ins., red-amber. £75-£100.

50. **Ridakoff.** 5 ins., aqua. £5-£7.

51. **Robinsons** bronchial cure, Baildon. 4 ins., light blue. £7-£10+.

52. **Dr. Rookes** rheumatic lixile. Cobalt blue. £7-£10.

53. **Ruby** remedy that cures. Round ended cylinder, 4 3/4 ins., clear. £3+.

54. **Sally-come-up** cures coughs & colds. 5 3/4 ins., aqua-blue. £10+.

55. **Scruttons** cough cure. Aqua-blue. £7-£10.

56. **Shawyers** Swindon express cough cure. 3 3/4 ins., aqua. £5+.

57. **Dr.Sibleys** solar tincture. Approx 7 ins. tall, clear, pontilled. £500+.

58. **Dr. Slades** cough & asthma cure, Perkin, Tamworth. 5 1/4 ins., aqua-green £5.

59. **Storcrofts** throat and chest cure. 6 1/4 ins., aqua. £3-£5.

60. **C. H. Talbots** pain curer, Boston & Spalding. 6 ins., aqua. £7-£10.

61. **Venos** lightning cough cure. 5 1/4 ins., aqua, very common. Pence!

62. **Venos** lightning cough cure. 5 1/4 ins., amber £15-£20+.

63. **Wands** cough cure. 5 ins., aqua £3+.

64. **Warners** safe cure, London. 4 1/2 ins., sample, amber £200-£250.

65. **Warners** safe cure, London. 7 1/4 ins., 1/2 pint amber. £10-£15.

66. **Warners** safe cure, London. 9 1/4 ins., pint green £30+.

67. **Warners** safe cure, London. 2 pint - referred to as 'Animal Cure', green. £250+.

68. **Warners** safe diabetes cure, London. 1 pint green £70-£100.

69. **Warners** log cabin extract. 8 ins., amber. £50-£70.

70. **Warners** safe nervine, London. 1/2 pint amber £20+.

71. **Warners** rheumatic cure, London. 1 pint, amber. £40-£50.

72. **Warners** tippecanoe. Round, embossed dug-out indian canoe, amber. £50-£70.

73. **Wessells** genuine jessuit drops, Shaw & Edwards, no. 67 St. Pauls Sq., 2 3/4 ins., pontilled. £40-£50+.

74. **Woods** great peppermint cure. 5 ins., aqua-green £2+.

COLEMAN'S NERVLETTES.

THE RAPID NERVE CURE

TO CURE THE BLUES

"**A FIT OF THE BLUES**" is one of the commonest ailments which afflicts humanity. Everybody feels "out of sorts" at times, and a remedy which will eradicate this very unpleasant feeling is simply invaluable. COLEMAN'S "NERVLETTES" are unsurpassable in their invigoration of the entire nervous system : the nerves are braced, the energies stimulated, the heart beats stronger, and the circulation of purified blood is vigorously increased.

COLEMAN'S "NERVLETTES" are sold by all Chemists, Stores, and Medicine Venders at 1/1½, 2/9, or 4/6 per bottle; but if at all difficult to procure, send stamps direct to the

PROPRIETORS: **J. CHAPMAN & Co. Ltd., NORWICH.**

What makes quacks particularly interesting are the often wonderful claims that they cure ALL. Sometimes the bottles themselves are rather plain, but the original adverts' help bring them to 'life'. Hugh Munden's advert', shown above, of 1906 suggests that Nervlettes are beneficial to the troops, think how they would help uplift you? Note how the soldiers already 'medicated' are smiling, having cured their blues!

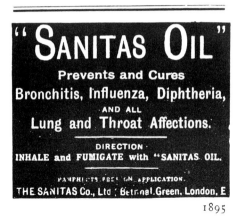
YOUR KIDNEYS ARE WEAK!

Kidney, Bladder and Uric Acid Troubles Make People Miserable.

Dr. Kilmer's Swamp-Root, the Great Kidney and Bladder Remedy, Will Overcome Such Troubles.

STONE IN THE BLADDER.

The cut below is taken from a photograph, and represents some of the specimens of gravel or stone passed from the bladder while taking Dr.

(3 Ounces and 27 Grains of Dissolved Stone or Gravel.)

Kilmer's Swamp-Root.

The following is a *verbatim copy* of a letter sent to Dr. Kilmer & Co., together with the *gravel or dissolved stone* as shown above. Mr. Bowersmith says:

" I doubt if there is a person living who can recommend your Swamp-Root more highly than myself. I had been a great sufferer from stone in the bladder, inflammation of the bladder, and kidney complaint, and was under the care of different physicians·for nearly two years. I tried every doctor

DR. KILMER'S
SWAMP-ROOT
Kidney, Liver & Bladder
REMEDY.
DIRECTIONS.
MAY TAKE one, two or three teaspoonfuls before or after meals and at bedtime.
Children less according to age.
May commence with small doses and increase to full dose or more, as the case would seem to require.

This Remedy is for Acute and Chronic Kidney, Liver, Bladder and Urinary Disorders, which often lead to Bright's Disease,
Pain in Back, Joints, Bones, or Rheumatism. It seldom fails to regulate a disordered liver. It is pleasant to take.
PREPARED ONLY BY
DR. KILMER & CO.,
BINGHAMTON, N. Y.
Sold by all Druggists.

DOULTON

MANVFACTVRERS · OF · GENERAL · STONEWARE · DRAIN PIPES · SANITARY · APPLIANCES · ARCHITECTVRAL · &

John Doulton was born in Fulham a small village on the Thames in 1793 and served his apprenticeship from 1805-1812 at the pottery founded by Dwight.

In 1812 he went to work for a small pottery at Vauxhall Walk where three years later he acquired an interest in the firm. (Jones, Watts and Doulton). By 1820 the pottery was owned by Doulton and Watts only and they expanded into larger premises in 1826, at Lambeth High Street.

The early products from this pottery were mainly ordinary salt-glazed blacking, ink and beer bottles and jugs, but also spirit flasks were mad ein the form of fishes, pistols, powder horns (reform flasks) together with dog and bird whistles, money-boxes and small replicas of constables' truncheons. There were impressed with the name Doulton & Watts after 1826.

Doulton & Watts made a wide range of reform flasks depicting politicians of the day connected with the Reform Act. These bottles were very popular and similar items were made to celebrate the Catholic Emancipation Act and the new Queen Victoria and her Prince Consort.

As the firm expanded it produced more utilitarian products such as filters, chemical vessels, drainpipes and eventually sanitary ware.

In 1854 with the retirement of John Doulton, a new partnership was formed under the name "Doulton & Co." which was ran by his son Henry, who had previously formed Henry Doulton Co. in 1848.

Henry Doulton continued to expand the firm exhibiting at the 1862 Exhibition and in 1877 acquired an interest in a firm in Burslem which in 1882 became Doulton & Company, Burslem, he died in 1897.

In 1899 a limited company was formed and two years later King Edward VII conferred a Royal Warrant on the Chairman and granted the firm the rare privilege of using the word "Royal" on its products.

The Lambeth Works were closed in 1956. By a series of mergers culminating with the Allied English Potteries Group in 1968, Doulton & Co., is today the largest manufacturer of ceramic products in the U.K. and even its modern products of to-day are eagerly sought after by collectors around the world.

Elliss's bulk ginger beer dispenser. A 20 inch ginger beer shape with tap hole facility at the bottom. Top and bottom portion glazed brown. Note above taphole 'Doultons Patent Secure Tap Jar' and the 'Doulton Lambeth' transfer mark below the main transfer. £120-£150+.

50

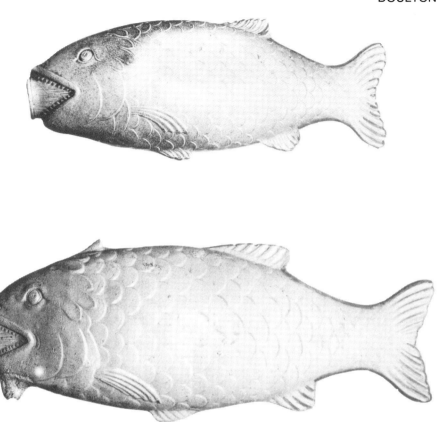

Three salt-glazed stoneware fish spirit flasks; 8 1/2 " to 11 1/2 " long, Doulton & Watts, Lambeth, early nineteenth century - £150-£200+. (Collection of Peter Doulton).

51

Rare Doulton two-tone salt-glazed whisky jug, "Col. Bogey Whisky". £500-£600+.

Display of Doulton Lambeth made stoneware ginger beer bottles in a variety of finishes; Bristol glaze, two-tone & salt-glaze, all embodying the undeniable Doulton quality transfers. Prices of these ginger beers vary from £20-£50+ but appear to be attracting increasing interest.

Highly desirable Doulton miniature water filter, value £500+.

Assortment of Doulton miniatures ranging in price from the plain mini g.b., £10-£15, up to the water filter £500+.

CHICAGO EXHIBITION, 1893. DOULTON & CO. HAVE OBTAINED
SEVEN HIGHEST AWARDS, THE LARGEST NUMBER GRANTED TO ANY FIRM OF POTTERS
IN THE WORLD.

Doulton & Co.

HEAD OFFICES & SHOW ROOMS, LAMBETH, S.E.

WORKS	DEPOTS
LAMBETH, LONDON	BIRMINGHAM.
ROWLEY REGIS, STAFF	LIVERPOOL.
ST. HELENS, LANCS.	MANCHESTER.
SMETHWICK	PARIS.
BURSLEM	
PAISLEY	
PARIS	

103 DIPLOMAS OF HONOUR GOLD MEDALS
AND FIRST CLASS AWARDS.

101 SILVER MEDALS
AND OTHER AWARDS.

TELEGRAPHIC ADDRESS,
"DOULTON, LONDON".
TELEPHONE No 4621.

In your reply

give this reference.

Lambeth Pottery,
London, S.E.
4th Feby 1896

Dear Reader,

We beg to inform you that further examples of our other products appear in this Volume on the following pages:—

6..., 7..., 79..., 80..., 100..., 101..., 102..., 103..., 127..., 128..., 155..., 156..., 157..., 158..., 180..., 182..., 184..., 187..., 193..., 195..., 198.

We are,

Yours respectfully,

Doulton & Co

Facsimile of Doulton Heading Paper 1896 used as index.

EYE BATHS

The medical profession developed small glass or ceramic vessels for liquid medication, or cleansing fluid, to be applied to tired, weary or poorly eyes.

The early types, 15th/16th century, were usually made of metal, silver types were recorded in the 16th/17th centuries, by the 18th century ornamental pottery, porcelain, types were found.

The 19th century saw a rapid growth in medication of all kinds and blown and moulded eye baths became the order of the day, for the masses, finally mass produced automatic machine models – produced to meet demands using the latest labour-efficient machinery.

We now rely on rubber replacements – nowhere near as pretty as the coloured glass examples which are now so very very popular.

1. Unstemmed, clear £1+.
2. Unstemmed, green £3-£5.
3. Unstemmed, blue £3-£5+.
4. Stemmed, blown/moulded type, cobalt blue. £7-£10+.
5. Stemmed, blown/moulded type, amber. £30-£50+.
6. Stemmed, blown/moulded type, puce. Rare. £75+.

7. Stemmed, blown/moulded type, emerald green. £5-£10.
8. Red - reference has been made over this colour, but not yet seen! £100+.
9. Plain ceramic type £10-£15+.
10. Earthenware, stemmed, blue & white decoration. Rare. £250-£1,000+.

EYE BATHS—

Fig. 254.

Fig. 255.

Fig. 256.

Fig. 257.

					per doz.
Earthenware, for N.H.I., Fig. 254	..	..	..	..	1/6
Glass, Turned in Rim, assorted colours, Fig. 255	..	..	..	..	2/3
,, ,, ,, ,, ,, Best Quality	..	..	..	..	3/3
,, with Reservoir, Polished Edges, Fig. 256	..	..	..	..	2/9
India Rubber, Grimes' Patent, Fig. 257	..	..	..	..	12/-

56

Figurals

Above right; 'Bears' trio; (Kummel liqueur) dark amethyst/black £40 to £60+, small aqua (complete with label written in Russian!) £100+, milk glass £40-£50+.

A. 4" - Dark aqua applied lip, small bubble burst on side. £5+. B. 1 3/4" - Cobalt Blue - screw top. £7-£10. C. 3" - Green - applied lip. £5+. D. 2" - Light blue milk-glass - screw top, reg. no. 791841. £7-£10. E. 2 1/2" - Milk glass applied lip. £25-30+. F. Blackpool Tower - clear glass. £12-£15. G. Eiffel Tower - clear glass embossed on base: "DISTILLERIE SERRES TOULOUSE FRANCE" Small chip on lip. £10+. H. Scarred base - clear glass - shear top full of dried tobacco? Policeman? £30-£40. I. Alces glass pontilled bottom. £50-£75. J. Vaseline - colour - scent bottle applied flared lip. £50-£60.

Fire Grenades

"Fire! Fire!"
In Victorian days, the memories of the Great Fire of London of 1666 still smouldered as a reminder of the devastation that fire can cause.

The ever ingenious inventors came up with the glass 'grenades' which were thrown into the flames, broke upon impact, and distributed their contents of carbon tetrachloride (or water mixed with carbon dioxide acid) to douse, or put out, the fire.

In 1871 the Harden Hand Fire Extinguisher Company of Chicago patented their first grenade. Today theirs is the most frequent type found, sure testament to the success of the Company.

The vivid colours of cobalt blue, greens, browns, turquoise, aqua, clear, combined with decorative projections combine to appeal to the nostalgic-hungry collector. Whether complete with contents, sealed with cement or wax, or empty, they are not easy items to discover, especially in original wire racks of twos or threesomes, to be wallhung in hotels, theatres, factories, or public places. It is possible to give added interest to a display with a few fire-fighting go-withs, related material, advertisements etc.

'Guru' of English fire grenade collectors is Ron Long, seen here with his wife and impressive display he put on at the 1985 Winternational.

L. cobalt 'P' grenade, type 9, with attractive raised dots all over surface. £200-£300. R. light amber 'Swift Fire Grenade', type 11, with t.m. in circle above. £100+.

L. taller than most is type 10 the cobalt labelled 'Sinclair Hand Grenade'. £40+. R. type 8 dark brown 'Merryweather, London'. £100+.

FIRE GRENADES

A rare pair of 'Imperial Fire Extinguishers', type 6, in original wall hanging bracket. £150-£200+.

L. green 'Imperial Fire Extinguisher', type 6, all lettering enclosed in a buckled belt design. £70+. R. type 5, amber 'Haywards Hand Fire Grenade'. £40-£50.

1. 'Firex', plain deep blue, with original cardboard box. £20+.
2. 'Hardens Star Grenade', cobalt blue, 2 raised vertical bands. Star T.m. £30+.
3. As previous but in original wire rack holding three. £120-£150+.
4. 'Hardens Star' 15 ins to 17 ins long tubular cylinder, raised bands etc. Rare. £200+.
5. 'Haywards Fire Grenade', amber, facetted. £40-£50.
6. 'The Imperial Fire Extinguisher', green, lettering within buckled belt. £70+.
7. As previous, but in original metal rack holding two. £150-£200.
8. 'Merryweather, London', deep brown, raised horizontal bands all around. £100+.
9. 'P' hand grenade. Cobalt blue, raised dots/pimples all over. Rare. £200-£300.
10. 'Sinclair & Co. Fire Grenade', cobalt blue, two raised circular bands with criss cross pattern between, with original paper label incorporating address. £40+.
11. 'Swift Fire Grenade', light amber, raised horizontal rings all over. £100+.

'The Firex' plain cobalt blue fire extinguisher, made interesting with the addition of the original box. On their own the glass grenades have, on occasion, been mistaken for target balls! £20+ (type 1).

Fire granades l to r.
Cobalt blue type 10 "Sinclair & Co. Fire Grenade" £40+. Type 5 "Haywards Fire Grenade", amber £40-£50. Type 2 "Hardens Star Grenade", blue - £30+, type 4 "Hardens Star Tube" - £200+.

GINGER BEERS

Transfer printed ginger beers from the late Victorian/early Edwardian period remain the number one collecting preoccupation of U.K. bottle collectors. It is a combination of several factors which easily explains this phenomenon – local interest/variation of shapes and colours/detailed pictorial transfers etc.

Our forefathers must have consumed vast quantities of the ginger beer beverage judging by the amounts of empty receptacles dug during the last one and and a half decades and now so proudly displayed in collections, and on stalls, for sale, in goodly numbers. Certainly their strength of manufacture has aided their survival over years of burial in long forgotten dumps.

Beginners to the hobby turn quickly to the better items, and this adds greatly to the demand for the best pictorials and rarities, thus continuing the upward trend in prices. However, whilst £325 may be the ceiling so far paid for an English g.b., the commoner items can still be picked up for a few pounds – and rapidly becoming antiques in the true sense of the word!

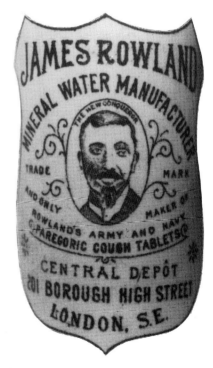

The visual appeal of quality detailed pictorial transfers makes ginger beers so highly collectable, and will undoubtedly continue to ensure their No. 1 slot in the popularity stakes?

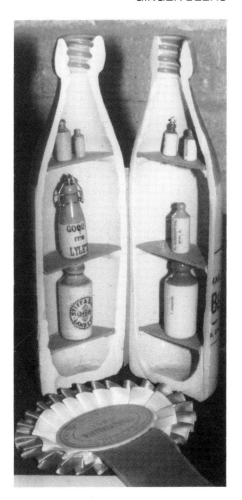

Together on shelves ginger beers offer a multitude of detail and interest, even to the non-collector. Shown above is a display at the first ever Glasgow Bottle Show, including many Scottish rarities. Scotland is renowned for quality pictorials, and a unique range of coloured lips and transfers.

Above; One of the most impressive competition entries seen at an English bottle show has to be this first prize winner of Bert Latham's at the 1982 Winternational. It features a large ginger beer cleverly sliced in half, and incorporating eight miniature examples.

Left; It is known that a few firms made pottery beakers, from which to drink their beverage, both in the U.K. and in America. However, such 'go-withs' are extremely rare, and all recorded feature identical transfers found on their sister ginger beers.

Above; As detailed a transfer found anywhere on a ginger beer bottle, though this is in fact for jug lager, and it extols its virtues too, '...exhiliarating, stimulating, rejuvenating, wholesome, delicious and pure'. Who could, indeed, resist it? Right; A 'R. Ellis' skittle shaped ginger beer from the North Wales town of Ruthin. Only a handful of these are known, all apparently having been dug from a South Wales site. This example also records 'Doulton Lambeth' at the base of the transfer. £250+.

Above L. to R; type 14 £3-£5, type 16 £50-£100, type 20 £10-£12, unique (?) variant of type 23 £75-£100.

1   **T. F. Adams & Son,** Halstead, ch., t.t., p.t.m. of flowers. £7-£10.
2.   **Armstrong & Son,** Lintz Green, ch., t.t, p.t.m. of steam train. £15+.
3.   **Arnold & Co.,** Lincoln, st., t.t., p.t.m. of Monks Abbey. £20+.
4.   **W. Atkinson & Son,** Helmsley, ch., t.t., p.t.m. of Helmsley castle. £30+.
5.   **Blackpool** Mineral Water Supply Ltd., ch., t.t., L, p.t.m. of Blackpool Tower. £40-£50+.
6.   **W. Brown,** Melrose, st., t.t., L., p.t.m. of Melrose Abbey. £200+.
7.   **Bullard & Sons,** Norwich, st., t.t., anchor t.m. £3-£5.
8.   **Caley,** Norwich & London. st., t.t., t.m. of crown. £3-£5.
9.   **Geo. Cammack,** Ormskirk, ch., t.t., p.t.m. of a two-towered church. £150-£200.
10.   **C.A.M.W.A.L.,** Harrogate. st., t.t. £3-£5.
11.   **G.T. Chadwick,** Rochdale. st., t.t., p.t.m. of dog £7-£10.
12.   **F. Chitty,** Chichester. st., all white, p.t.m. of castle. £7-£10.
13.   **Claytons,** Cardiff. st., dark brown top., £3-£5.
14.   **Claytons,** London & Kingston. st., t.t., c.c. £3-£5.
15.   **J. Orr Comrie.** ch., green lip and transfer. Small p.t.m. of bowman. £35-40+.
16.   **Comrie & Co.,** Helensburgh. st., t.t., all white, p.t.m. of jovial drinking man. £50-£60.

17.   **Wm. Corry & Co.,** Belfast. st., t.t., blue transferred p.t.m. of phoenix. £40-£50.
18.   **T. Cook & Son,** Folkestone & Dover. ch., t.t., p.t.m. of foaming glass. £75-£100.
19.   **Coomb Spring,** Milford Haven. ch., t.t., p.t.m. of harp. £100-£120+.
20.   **Cooper & Co.,** Glasgow, Liverpool & London. st., all white, p.t.m. of 2 coopers. £10-£12.
21.   **Austin Craven,** Manchester. st., light brown, p.t.m. of fisherman. £10-£12.
22.   **The Crewe Mineral Water Co.** st., t.t., p.t.m. of steam train & tender. £12-£15.
23.   **M. Denwood & Sons,** Carlisle. st., t.t., p.t.m. of Queen Victoria. £75-£100.
24.   **Dornat & Co.,** Barnstaple & Devon. st., all white, p.t.m. of tree. £3-£5.
25.   **Duncan Flockhart & Co.,** Grimsby & London. ch., t.t. £12-15+.
26.   **Economic Supply Co.,** Grimsby & London. ch., t.t., p.t.m. of albatross and anchor. £250.
27.   **Edinburgh & Leith** Aerated Water Co. ch., t.t., L. £15-20+.
28.   **Edmondson & Co., Ltd.,** Liverpool. ch., t.t., p.t.m. of girl on swing. £70-£80.
29.   **R. Emmerson & Co.,** Newcastle-on-Tyne. ch., t.t., p.t.m. of man on penny farthing. £25-£30.
30.   **Emmersons 'Factory".** ch., t.t., p.t.m. of factory. £250-£300+.

GINGER BEERS

A mouth watering selection of predominantly Welsh ginger beers, put on by Garry Higgins, one of the countries leading coloured-top specialists, at the 1982 Dorking Bottle Show.

This competition entry by Mike Smith shows the range of closure patents taken out by the pottery manufacturers. Apart from the Atherons piece, second from right, all of these would be very difficult to track down. The blue top blue transfer Galtee More patent, 'Hart & Co., Nottingham', rates as one of the best three ginger beers available anywhere in the world - £500+?

Above L. to R; type 26 £250, type 29 £25-£30, type 36 £7-£10, type 47 £400-£500.

31.	**W. Everett,** Cromer, st., t.t. £7-£10.
32.	**Firths,** Darlington, st., t.t., blue transfer p.t.m. of locomotive. £15-20.
33.	**H. Firth,** Manningham. st., all white, p.t.m. of sailing ship £7-£10.
34.	**Forrest & Co.,** Inverness. ch., t.t., p.t.m. of building. £7-£10.
35.	**Furgusons,** Plymouth. st., all white, blue transfer. £7-£10.
36.	**Green & Ledicott,** Southend, st., t.t., orange top. £7-£10.
37.	**Goulds, King & Barnes,** Horsham. st., green top £30+.
38.	**Halls Ltd.,** Walkden. ch., t.t., p.t.m. of cockerel £15-£20.
39.	**Hancocks,** Wiveliscombe. st., all cearam. £3-£5.
40.	**Harston & Co.,** Leeds & Harrogate. st., honey, p.t.m. of bird. £5-£8.
41.	**J. Hegginbotham,** Stalybridge. st., blue top £3-£5..
42.	**Robert Henderson,** Westoe Brewery, South Shield. ch., t.t., large pictorial t.m. of negro drinking. £80-£100.
43.	**William Hodgson,** Blackburn. st., t.t., p.t.m. of St. Paul (?) £7-£10+.
44.	**Hoopers,** Pall Mall East London & Brighton. st., honey £5+.
45.	**Idris.** st., t.t., lettering in script £3-£5.

46.	**Chas. B. Inman,** Leeds, Knaresboro. st., t.t., p.t.m. of sculpted figure £7-£10+.
47.	**Geo. Jeff & Co.,** Hull. ch., all white, p.t.m. of Imp. £400-£500.
48.	**James Jeffrey,** Aberdeen. ch., t.t., p.t.m. of fireman. £25-£30.
49.	**W. G. Johnstone & Co.,** Dumfries. st., t.t. £3-£5.
50.	**J. Kerswall,** Exeter. st., light brown, figural p.t.m. £20+.
51.	**C. Kimber,** Rotherham, ch., t.t £7-£10.
52.	**Laycocks,** chester. st., t.t., p.t.m. of lion £15-£20.
53.	**G. Lawrence & Sons,** Norfolk. Reverse t.t., very many variations - commonest £5-£8.
54.	**Lauterback,** Sunderland. ch., t.t., p.t.m. of two crossed keys £150-200.
55.	**Lemon & Co.,** Dingwall. st., t.t. £10-£15.
56.	**Licensed Trade Supply Co. Ltd.,** Coventry. £7-£10.
57.	**George Low,** Montrose, ch., t.t., p.t.m. of shop premises. £300.
58.	**Macdonald Bros.,** Dufftown. ch., t.t., p.t.m. of piper. £10+.
59.	**A. W. Mackintosh Bros.,** ch., t.t., p.t.m. of highlander & two bottles. £25-£30.
60.	**Martins,** Grantham. ch., t.t. £3-£5.
61.	**Mason & Burrows,** Manchester. st., honey (also sold whisky?) £3-£5.

GINGER BEERS

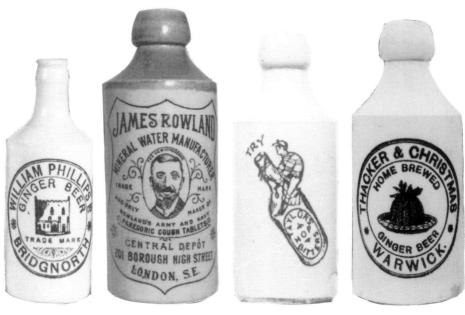

Above L to R; type 74 £7-£10, type 83 £75-£100, type 96 £75+, type 97 £25-£30.

Above L to R; type 98 £50-£75, type 104 £150-£200, type 109 £40-£50, type 112 £120-£150.

Above L to R; type 49 £3-£5, type 65 £120-£150, type 71 £30+, type 72 £150+.

62.   **W. B. Mew Langton,** Newport, I.O.W. st., all white, p.t.m. of horse £7-£10.

63.   **J. Mills & Son,** London. st., t.t., beehive top, t.m. shield £12-15+.

64.   **Milnes & Son,** Bradford. ch., t.t., p.t.m. of boy on donkey. £25-£30+.

65.   **Morrison & Townend,** Castleford. st., t.t., p.t.m. of talking man. £120-£150.

66.   **Mumbys,** Portsmouth. st., t.t., c.c. £3-£5.

67.   **Niblett & Cos.,** Stroud & Cheltenham. st., t.t. £3-£5.

68.   **Norman.** st., blue blob top. £7-£10.

69.   **North & Randall,** Aylesbury. st., blue top, p.t.m. of monument. £30-£40.

70.   **Oak Aerated Water Co.,** Wigan. ch., t.t., p.t.m. of oak tree £25-£30+.

71.   **Pain & Bayles,** Ipswich & Felixstowe. st., t.t., p.t.m. of turret. £30+.

72.   **Parsons & Co.,** Blackheath. st., t.t., p.t.m. of elaborate building. £150+.

73.   **Dave Phillips & Pett Ltd.,** Rochester. st., t.t., p.t.m. of female bust. £25-£30.

74.   **William Phillips,** Bridgnorth. st., all white, p.t.m. of building £7-£10.

75.   **Premier Table Water Co. Ltd.,** New Brighton. st., t.t., large p.t.m. of lighthouse. £150.

76.   **Probyns,** Gold medals. st., t.t., p.t.m. of lady amidst shrubbery £30-£50.

77.   **Randall & Sons,** Chesterfield. ch., t.t., p.t.m. of twisted spire. £30+.

78.   **Reigate Brewery.** st., t.t., p.t.m. of castle £40-£50.

79.   **J. E. Richardson,** Yarmouth. ch., t.t., p.t.m. of three masted schooner. £60-£75.

80.   **Rimmington & Son,** Bradford. st., t.t., p.t.m. of apothecary. £15-£20+.

81.   **Robertsons,** Oban. ch., t.t., sepia transferred p.t.m. of deer. £80-£100.

82.   **W. & H. Roome,** Darlington. st., t.t., p.t.m. of head -on sailing ship. £80-£100.

83.   **James Rowland,** London. st., t.t., p.t.m. of moustachioed mans head. £75-£100.

84.   **Robert Ryder,** St. Helens. ch., t.t., blue transfer of pit winding gear. £80-£100.

85.   **Sang & Co.,** Elgin. ch., L., blue transfer, p.t.m. of two-turreted church. £200-£250.

86.   **G. T. Scott & Co.,** Wallsend ch., t.t., p.t.m. of Father Tyne. £75-£100.

87.   **E. P. Shaw & Co.,** Wakefield. st., t.t., p.t.m. of dog. £5-£10.

88.   **Skene Dufftown.** ch., t.t., c.c., p.t.m. of piper £10-£12.

89.   **Sketches,** Pembroke Dock. st., green top. £35-£40.

90.   **W. Southern,** Belper. ch., t.t., p.t.m. of three storied shop front. £35-£50.

91.   **Steward & Pattison Ltd.,** Norwich & Swafham. st., brown, ld t.m. £3-£5.

GINGER BEERS

A range of 'foreigners'. Though interest in overseas ginger beer is, generally, luke-warm some of the pictorials do have a following. This is not really surprising when you consider that the majority were in fact made here. Some may never have left our shores, others may have come back as ballast in ships?

92. **William Stones,** Sheffield. ch., t.t., p.t.m. of strongman lifting a cannon. £30-£40.

93. **R. Stothert,** Atheron. ch., t.t., p.t.m. of bearded man. £60-£90.

94. **Sullivans** (South African g.b.) ch., t.t., L., p.t.m. of mans head. £75-£90.

95. **Tamplin & Co.,** Liverpool. ch., t., p.t.m. of Liver bird. £30-£40.

96. **Taylors Hop Bitters,** Manchester. st. all cream, p.t.m. of jockey on bottle. £75+.

97. **Thacker & Christmas,** Warwick. st., all white, p.t.m. of Christmas pud. £25-£30.

98. **James M. Todd,** Kirkcaldy, st., t.t., p.t.m. of tower. £50-£75.

99. **Torquay Mineral Water Co.,** Torquay. st., all white. £3-£5.

100. **Turnbull,** Hawick. st., t.t. £7-£10.

101. **W. Underwood,** Carlisle. ch., t.t., L., p.t.m. of factory. £120-£150.

102. **Vallance,** Sidmouth, ch., green top, L. £40-£50.

103. **Victoria Wine Co.,** London. st., t.t., p.t.m. of young Queen Victorias head. £40+.

104. **Watson & Beckwith,** Spennymor. ch., t.t., p.t.m. full male figure. £150-£200.

105. **R. Whites,** Windsor. st., t.t. £3-£5.

106. **M. Whittacker,** Matlock Bath. ch., t.t. £7-£10.

107. **Wilson & Bates,** Glossop. ch., t.t., p.t.m. of large dragon. £50-£75.

108. **Job Wragg,** Birmingham. st., all white p.t.m. of soda syphon. £7-£10.

109. **W. H. Wood,** Durham. ch., t.t., p.t.m. of Durham Cathedral £40-£50.

110. **Wrexhams.** st., t.t., p.t.m. of goat. £15-£20+.

111. **Y.A.B.C.,** Gt. Yarmouth. st., blue top, rather plain. £25-£30.

112. **Yorkshire Fermented Drinks Co.,** Leeds. st., all white, p.t.m. of bisons head. £120-£150.

113. **Youngs,** Crawshay & Young, diss. st., t.t. £5-£8.

114. **Youngman Preston & Co.,** Lowestoft. st., t.t., p.t.m. of small eagle. £30-£40.

Left; 'The Golden Malt & Hop Nourishing Stout ... uniquely features a list of five of its distribution depots. The beer dray pictorial is also featured on their beer bottles, but, as is so often the case, the t.m. is much larger – to the dismay of ginger beer collectors!

Below; Advertisement from the Mineral Water Makers Manual of 1892 showing two salt glaze g.b.'s.

BOURNE'S

CELEBRATED

STONE BOTTLES

FOR

GINGER BEER.

JOSEPH BOURNE & SON,

Manufactory—

DENBY POTTERY, near DERBY.

London Warehouse and Offices—

NEW ST. PANCRAS STATION, EUSTON RD., N.W.

Above; Two of the most desirable pottery advertising ginger beers. Left; Blue top champagne shape 'Price Powell & Co'. Right; Blue top standard shape 'Price Sons & Co' with ble transfer and galtee more patent hole in neck (patented in 1897). Both items strictly "price by negotiation".

Gins

Holland's most famous export has to be its renowned gin. From the 17th century their now familiar square gin bottles, tapering inwards towards the base, were encased in pompartmentalised wooden crates (hence their square shape!) for their journey worldwide. By the late 1700's 14 million gallons of gin was produced in the Netherlands region.

The distinctive shaped 'case bottles', with many subtle variations in size and colour, carried on right up to the present day, are now avidly collected in Australia, the U.S. and, more and more, in the U.K.

L. to R., back row; type 5 £30-£40, type 2 £60-£80, type 3 £15-£20 and type 10 £5+. Front row; two type 4's £10+.

Quite scarce 6 1/2 ins. pontilled free-blown, olive green glass, rectangular body. The applied seal shown in detail alongside featuring the Star of David and a fish. (Type 6) £50-£75.

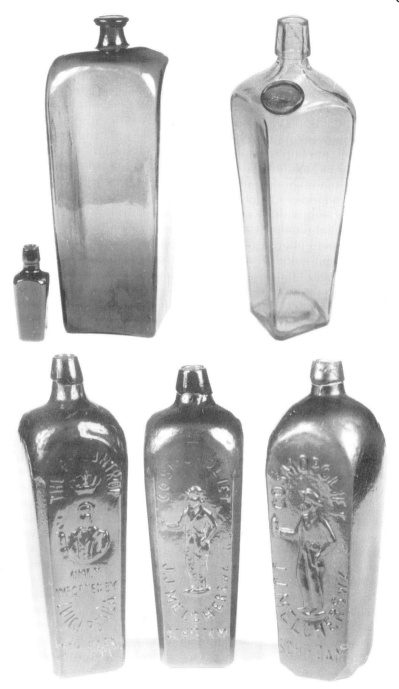

Top L.; type 4 mini unembossed £10+, alongside a 15 ins free-blown £50+. R; type 9, cobalt seal on a clear glass body £100. Bottom row; L. 'The Philanthrop' (type 8) pictorial black glass £200-£250, with two variations of the 'Cosmopoliet' on its R (type 7). £100-£120.

GINS

1. Free-blown, pontilled, flared lip, olive green, 18 ins. £200-£250+.
2. Free-blown, pontilled, flared lip, olive green, very thin walls, neck slightly depressed, 10 1/2 ins. £60-£80.
3. Free-blown, olive green, 8 1/2 ins., not so crude, deep aqua. £15-£20.
4. Unembossed, 4 ins., 5 ins., or 6 ins. olive green mini. £10+.
5. 'AVH' shoulder sealed gin. Embossed down one panel 'A Van Hoboken, Rotterdam', 11 ins. +, brown/green. £30-£40.
6. Rectangular bodied sealed free-blown. Star of David and fish on seal. Green and brown, 9 ins. Scarce. £50-£75.
7. 'The Cosmopoliet, J. J. Melchers, Schiedam' embossed with full figure of man drinking. Dark glass in 8 1/2 ins. and 10 1/2 ins. sizes. £100-£120.
8. 'The Philanthrop, Demerara', 10 1/2 ins., very dark glass, embossed picture of mans head and shoulders. Rare. £200-£250.
9. 'Schiedam', clear glass shape with applied cobalt seal. Rare. £100.
10. 'Ploopuy & Co.' circa 1900 type, embossed case, deep green/brown. £5+.
11. Later pictorials, a very extensive range available; Buffalo, Warthog, Knight on Horseback, jackal, etc. usually green, but reducing down to aqua. £30-£100+.
12. Anchor pictorial. Early type with chamferred basal cornerls embossed 'T. H. C. & Co., Hollands', with picture of anchor. Very dark glass. Rare. £200+.

Above; Early black glass type, with typical chamferred basal corners, is believed to be the only one known? Embossed 'T. C. H. (entwined initials) & Co., Hollands' with large anchor t.m. Due to its slight water washed condition valued at £200+.

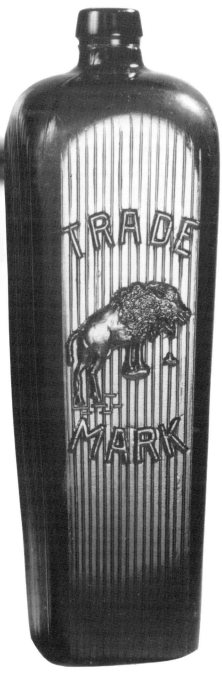 

Two examples from the extensive range of later-type pictorial gins. These vary from very deep greens through to light greens, even aqua. The Water Buffalo L. features vertical ribbing attributed to the mould marks and is a dark green bottle. £70-£100. R. a much lighter green pictorial without the prominent ribbing £50-£70.

Another contrasting pair of the later type pictorials. L. 'Knight on Horseback', very rare, featuring vertical mould lines, £50+. R. 'Jackal' in a darker green glass and more lightly struck mould lines £30+.

Hot=Water Bottles

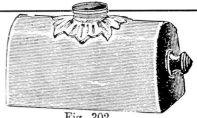

Fig. 302.

Stoneware,	Fig. 302			1 qt.	3 pt.	2 qt.	3 qt.
	Each	...	...	2/1	2/6	3/2	3 8

Before the days of central heating people relied upon heavy pottery hot water bottles to warm their beds, prior to kip. There are some quite early sprigged salt glaze types from the early 1800's, but they are rare. In bottle spheres most encountered are the later Victorian types, the transferred ones being the most popular. Poor folk made do with a large stone/pebble warmed in the oven and wrapped in a cloth!

The hobby has again benefited in this area by interest from interior designers/decorators quick to capitalize on the visual appeal of these warmers in modern settings – around the stone fireplace, or displayed in the bathroom? Pictorial transfers and the miniatures are especially in demand, their prices increasing the most during the last five years.

Old habits die hard and pottery footwarmers continued their useful lives long after the advent of the rubber footwarmers.

N.B. All the illustrations reproduced in this section are from an original May Roberts Druggists' Sundries Catalogue.

An amusing gathering of 'footwarmer folk' by Sue Davidson of the Surrey Bottle Collectors Club. The miniature types, in particular, are increasingly difficult to pick up.

HOT WATER BOTTLES

1. Small 'brick' shape, plain £5-£10.
2. Large 'brick' shape, plain £3-£5.
3. Early saltglaze 'brick' type, £20-£30.
4. Transferred 'Doultons improved Foot Warmer. £20+.
5. Miniature 'Made At Ye Olde Fulham Pottery'. £50-£70.
6. Large 'Adaptable' with front bung. £20-£30+.
7. Smaller 'Adaptable'. £20-£30+.
8. Tiny 'Adaptable' muff warmer complete with handle and stopper. £50-£70.
9. The 'carrier' brick type. £10+.
10. The 'Bungalow', rectangular. £30-£50.
11. The 'Arctic' picture of igloo, eskimos etc. £70-£100+.
12. The 'Little Folks', bedroom scene. 6 ins. by 6 ins. £70-£100+.
13. The 'Mecca' with green transfer. £30-£50.
14. The 'Mecca' with multicoloured Japanese style scene, rare. £100-£200.

The 'Arctic' was sold in 1 pint, 2 pint and 3 pint capacities, though we can only recall having seen one size? This is one of the rarer pictorials, type 11 £70-£100+.

The 'Little Folks' (type 12) apparently only produced in one 6 ins. by 6 ins. size. These cost 17/1d per dozen in 1925, though the most expensive were the 6 pint Adaptables at 40/2d per dozen. Today the 'Little Folks' command £70 to £100+ according to transfer quality.

The 'Mecca' is a lightly cast pottery item with a more porcelaneous quality 'feel' than the usual heavy stonewares, and features a green transfer. There is a much rarer multi-coloured version with Japanese style scenes (see BBR 28, page 6). (Type 13), £30-£50.

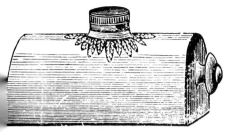

The familiar 'brick' shape, except this has applied sprigging around the top. The simple types range from £3 to £5, though the smaller ones fetch £5 to £10. Found in 1 1/2 pint, 3 pint and 1,2, and 4 quarts capacities. These are also available with carrying handles, called 'The Carrier'

Mini muff warmer, type 8, of 4 oz capacity. Falling in to the miniatures catergory, as this does, complete with handle and stopper they sell for £50 to £70, without either £20 to £25.

Doulton typically developed the brick shape and threw in their obligatory scrolled transfer. Judging by their abundance the 'Improved Foot Warmer' sold remarkably well, type 4, £20+.

The ' Adaptable' apparently sold in 4 oz, 1 pint, 2 pint, 3 pint, 4 pint and 6 pint capacities, the larger ones having the bung/filling hole at the front. Their demand, today, outside of bottle circles, means prices are ever creeping upwards. (Type 6 & 7) £20-£30+.

An attractive rectangular shaped warmer with idyllic bungalow in centre (type 10). It was sold in small, medium and large sizes though can only recall seeing 1 size in almost 15 years of bottling? The transfers vary considerably in quality and often the stopper is missing. £30 to £50+ if mint and complete, more if a local store name appears below the main transfer.

Doulton based their best selling transferred 'Improved Foot Warmer' on the well tried and loved simple 'brick' shape which had stood the test of time for so long. Typically they threw in swirly scrolls in their version. Shown above is a, now, rare advertising piece for G. Wyatts stores in Oxford. Type 4's often sell for £20+, but with local interest, such as this, collectors would willingly pay £30-£50.

Above; L. miniature Old Fulham Pottery muffwarmer with stopper, but sans handle, type 5, £50. R. base of another Doultons Improved type with small ad. for Wyatts Oxford stores. £70-£100+.

The introduction of India rubber bedwarmers saw the demise of the breakable old stoneware types. However, many have survived for to-days collectors, some are even still in use by elderly (and not so elderly?) folk.

INHALERS

In Christmas 1983 I underwent a nose operation. During my week long stay in hospital, I was amazed at the high stock of pottery transferred inhalers kept in the storeroom at the end of the ward, even more surprised that they were still in daily use.

For practical purposes they perform their function perfectly well, still, inhalation of medicinal vapours either for healing purposes or for clearing nasal blockages.

When Victorian extravagance was at its height, and the engravers art at a peak, a number of exceptionally attractive pieces were manufactured. Elaborately decorated in an effort, maybe, to hide their purpose?

Whilst the vase majority now available to the collectors are relatively mundane they still find homes – possibly fitting into general medical or cure related displays. The fine and elaborate items, some in blue, sepia, and purple transfers, have taken on a stature on a par with their massive increase in asking prices.

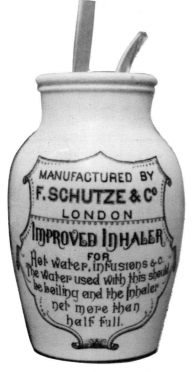

L. Rare 'F. Schultze & Co., London' fairly simple graphic lay-out on a different shaped body to most found £50+. R. Attractive 'Universal Inhaler' blue with black background mottling. £70-£100+.

THE OXFORD
INHALER.
HALF-FILL THE VESSEL WITH
THE INFUSION. TAKING
CARE THE BENT TUBE
DOES NOT TOUCH THE
CONTENTS. REPLACE
THE COVER & THE
INHALER IS READY
FOR USE.

TRADE MARK

Above; the magnificent 'Oxford Inhaler' with beautifully ornate sepia transfer of birds and foliage etc.
Surely the finest inhaler available, as well as being extremely rare. Type 4, £200-£300.

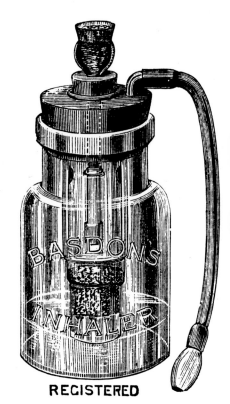

REGISTERED

Above; This dump dug 'The Perfect Inhaler' is a rare pictorial example from 'R. Sumner & Co., 50a Lord Street, Liverpool. 1995 price £100+.

It was entered in the auction at the 1985 British National weekend with a reserve of just £30. As testament to the level of interest now, in these rarer and more attractive pieces, the final hammer price was £65, though the postal bidders' limit was very much higher!

1. Simple Maws inhaler, with spout. £10+.
2. Maws double-valved, large type with bent neck. £40-£50.
3. Mottled-body Maws Improved, with spout. £40+.
4. The Oxford Inhaler, highly elaborate transfer featuring birds and foliage, sepia transfer. £200-£300.
5. The Perfect Inhaler, R. Sumner & Co., Liverpool. £100+.
6. F. Schutze & Co., London. £50+.
7. The Universal Inhaler, Bourne, Johnson & Latimer, London. Blue with black background mottling. £70-£100+.
8. The Westminster Inhaler, highly elaborate foliage transfer in sepia. £100-£200.

Interesting Inhalers of 1895 from ARNOLD & SONS, LONDON Medical Catalogue.

MAW'S
EARTHENWARE INHALERS
For Hot Water, Infusions, &c.

FIG. 8.

MAW'S IMPROVED.

FIG. 6.

MAW'S DOUBLE-VALVED.

FIG. 8A.

MAW'S IMPROVED.

Fig. 6.—Double-Valved, 60/- per dozen; with Elastic Tubes, 78/-

Fig. 8.—Marbled, 32/ per dozen.   Fig. 8a.—White, 21/- per dozen.

Fig. 8a.—White, half size, 13/- per dozen.

ELASTIC TUBES, with Mouthpieces, to fit Fig. 8 and 8a, 7 inches long, 8/- per dozen; 9 inches long, 12/- per dozen.

SPECIAL QUOTATIONS TO WHOLESALE BUYERS.

MANUFACTURED BY

S. MAW, SON & THOMPSON, LONDON.

Advertisement from "The Chemist and Druggists Diary 1889".

INKS

It is not difficult to understand the charm of the receptacles which once held ink. The age before the biro, when all writers, mostly learned folk, needed ink bottles of some sort to replenish regularly their quills, desk pots, or even one of the 'new fangled' fountain pens.

Imagine the impact the Governments 1870 compulsory education act had on the sale of ink, and the boost given for the containers used.

Glass sheared lip inks lent themselves to simple closure with cork and sealing wax. In a market rapidly becoming competitive manufacturers turned to ingenious patent designs and novel eye-catching shapes, in an attempt to capture a larger slice of the cake!

The more mundane items, so mass produced, are today valued for their crudeness, whilst the bright colours; – greens, ambers, blues etc., being much rarer add further to their collectability and, unfortunately, their value.

It has been claimed that in ink lies as varied a range as any other bottle category? Be that as it may, they remain ardently collected all over the world.

Left; 'House of Inks' by Portsmouth ink boffin Ashley McAvery. Right; a junior 'Well' entry of inks by a Norwich Club member at one of their annual Shows.

The ubiquitous cottage ink, much adored the world over. This particular example is the rare variant featuring a diamond registration mark, type no. 12, for April 5th 1869. Though cottages are not actually all that rare collectors are reluctant to part with good examples, even though they may not specialise or generally collect inks. As a result they remain difficult to pin-point, and relatively expensive. £250+.

INKS

Shape variations of fairly common aqua inks.

Top row, L. to R.; boat shape (type 4), three variations of cone shapes (type 9). Second row; unembossed cottage (type 10), 3 plain rounds (28). 3rd row; triangular 'Derby All British' (14), round tipper (39), and 2 plain squares (31). Bottom row; less common round type, and ocatagonal, square with ribs on three sides (32), and a circular tent with basal diamond registration mark.

Above; snail ink, aqua, in metal stand, type 34 - £40+. Not easy pieces to find, though some dilligent collectors manage to buy the two parts separately, eventually, and put together a complete one, for a fraction of the usual cost.

1. **Armchair** shaped ink, offset neck, aqua. £10-£15.
2. **Blackwoods Patent,** igloo shape, offset neck, aqua. £7-£10.
3. **Boot/shoe shape,** several variations, aqua or clear. £35-£50.
4. **Boat shape,** aqua. £1-£2.
5. **Boat shape,** amber. £30+.
6. **Boat shape,** cobalt. £15-£20.
7. **Birdcage,** aqua or clear. 30-£40.
8. **Barrel,** vertical ringed, clear. £7-£10+.
9. **Cone,** aqua. £2+.
10. **Cottage shape,** unembossed, aqua. £10-£15.
11. **Cottage shape,** two windows & door, rear nib recess, diamond roof. £60-£75.
12. **Cottage shape,** 2 windows & door, rear 2 windows and diam. reg. mark, rect. roof tiles, base embossed 'Regd. April 5 '69'. £250+.
13. **Daniel Lambert** (fat man), figural saltglaze, two quill holes. £500+.
14. **'Derby All British',** triangular, aqua. £3-£5.
15. **Flower shape** ink, (from above?), sheared lip, aqua. £20+.
16. **Hyde,** London, octagonal embossed down two panels, aqua. 3-£5.
17. **Hyde,** London, as above but green. £5+.
18. **Hyde,** London, tall elegant round shape, pouring lip aqua. £3-£5.
19. **Farrars 1 - V perfumed ink,** impressed circular saltglaze. £25-£30.
20. **Fields Ink & Gum,** square, aqua, a.b.m. £1.

21. **Fields Ink & Gum,** square, light amber, a.b.m. 20-£30.
22. **Fields Ink & Gum,** rd. no. 660693, square pottery, pouring lip. £3-£5.
23. **J. Field,** square, sheared lip, aqua. £2.
24. **Lions head figural,** saltglazed pottery. £70-£100.
25. **Monk,** holding bowl, pottery figural, salt glaze. £500-£700.
26. **Ma & Pa Carter,** coloured matching pottery pair, patented Jan 8th, 1914. £80-£100.
27. **Pridges Inks,** London N.E., 4 ins. white glaze, pouring lip. £5-£8.
28. **Round,** sheard lip, unembossed, aqua. 50p.
29. **Round,** brown, a.b.m. £20-£30.
30. **Shaws Inks Are The Best,** octagonal, embossed on 5 sides, aqua. £5-£7.
31. **Square,** aqua, sheared lip. 50p.
32. **Square,** aqua, sheared lip, ribbed three sides. £1.
33. **Square,** cobalt, sheared lip, ribbed three sides. £20+.
34. **Snail Ink,** in metal stand, aqua. £40+.
35. **Square necked,** orangey saltglaze, pouring lip, eg. diam., several sizes. £7-£10.
36. **Teakettle,** pottery, shiny brown, no other markings. £40-£50.
37. **Teakettle,** aqua glass, facetted body. £30-£50.
38. **Teakettle,** green glass, facetted. £150-£200.
39. **Tipper,** round, sheard lip, aqua. £3-£5.
40. **Ugly woman,** saltglaze. £50-£100.

Right; A colourful and amusing pair of matching Ma & Pa Carter inks (26). These were produced in Germany, patented Jan. 8th 1914, and used to test the power of advertising in a magazine in America. They proved quite popular, and remain equally as popular amongst todays ink collectors. £80-£100.

Above, L to R;- salt glazed variation of type 40 'Ugly Woman', more detailed than example shown opposite. Two teakettles, larger size mid blue with early type spout, the other mid green. Birdcage, type 7, £30-£40. Blackwoods, type 2, offest neck and diamond registration, £7-£10. Sunflower (?) ink £20+.

Above L., part of an enamel sign advertising Moncrieff's blue black writing ink, which depicts a fine labelled stoneware bulk container. These shapes are more often missing the highly attractive and sometimes colourful bit of paper. R. a screw stoppered bulk bottle, which originally cost £2/9d. Again complete with label, and this time contents as well.

Above; L. type 40, ugly woman, in saltglaze £50+ this type. R. a rare saltglazed Daniel Lambert, once the fattest man in early Victorian times, a variation on type 13. £500+.

KITCHENALIA

THE BEST THAT MONEY CAN BUY.

Borwick's Baking Powder.

The television series of the late 70's 'Upstairs Downstairs' gave millions of viewers an accurate insight into the gadgetry prevalent in a Victorian gentlemans kitchen.

Today Kitchenalia, the collecting of old kitchen items, goes way beyond the confines of bottles and has an enormous following. Anything from rolling pins to pie funnels, jam pots to jelly moulds comes under this heading, in tin, brass, wood, pottery etc.

We are, here, more concerned with the pottery or glass kitchen related artifacts that can be recovered from our richly diverse bottle dumps.

It is often the cas that "hubby" collects the more manly (?) ginger beers, wines etc., whilst the understanding, and part won-over, loving wife shows an interest in pieces to adorn her kitchen. Such items are real conversation makers amongst visitors and party guests.

Typical hunting grounds for 'Kitchenalia'; – bottle dumps, Bottle Shows, Antique Fairs & Shops, but be ever on the look-out, things appear in the most unexpected of places.

In future volumes of this Encyclopaedia we intend to expand on various facets within this broad category.

Original cardboard C.W.S custard powder container, £7-£10, alongside a transferred blancmange bowl complete with "how-to-do-it" instructions. This was dug on one of Yorkshire most productive tips in 1978. £10-£20.

1. **'Cairns Fairyland jams'.** Black transfer with coloured blackcurrants above. £75-£100.
2. **'Fletts Celebrated Blackcurrant, Liverpool'.** Two tone, impressed lettering picked out in brown. £10-£15.
3. **'Harris's Nourishing turtle soup, for invalids'.** Two tone, impressed lettering picked out in brown. £30-£50.
4. **'Joseph Holmes, Yorkshire Preserved Fruit Manufactory, Leeds'.** T.t., impressed lettering picked out in blue. £20+.
5. **'Hudson Brothers Marmalade, London & Provinces'.** Black transfer. £7-£10.
6. **'Kemps Extract of Chicken'**, small chicken pictorial, black trans. £10-£20.
7. **'G & C. Nuttall, Kingston on Thames'**, t.t., impressed lettering picked out in brown. £20-£30.
8. **'T. Pecriaux, turtle soup'**, T.t., pictorial, black transfer, 3 sizes. £100-£150.
9. **'R. Swifts Celebrated Ormskirk Brawn'**, pigs head pic., blue transfer. £40-£50+.
10. **'Wotherspoons Scotch Marmalade'**, early pot, with additional products advertised round sides. Black transfer. Rare. £50-£75+.

Not everyones collecting 'cup of tea' but, judging by the numbers which do come to light, Turtle Soup must have been a fairly popular Victorian delicacy? The above rare impressed example includes the rather dubious claim 'sticks to your ribs'? £30-£50.

The most commonly found Turtle Soup pot is that put out by T. Pecriaux, available in 3 transferred sizes, and more in the earlier slabbed/impressed version. Rarely dug they generally appear in Antique shops from time to time. £100-£150.

Marmalade pots in themselves are a quite extensive field in themselves, with some fine examples recorded. Most are the same shape, a few are pictorial, whilst rarer still are the coloured examples. The 'Fleets' example above is a rare item, the 'Cairns' pot has a black transfer with coloured blackcurrants and is the only one we have ever seen.

Over the years the larger firms, such as Lyles & Keillers, produced several variations in their transfers. Wotherspoons appear to be the only ones who struck on the novel idea of advertising other products on the empty space around the pot. The one above shows the front, and one side, promoting 'Glenfield Starch'. Unfortunately these are very rarely found in good condition. Type £50-£75.

Above;- L to R - **green lip** 10 oz 'Oldham Aerated Water Co.', owl pictorial codd, £150-£200. **Cobalt** stick bottle (Barrett & Elers type) 'Gilberd & Co., Napier (N.Z.) 1880', £150-£400 depending on density of the blue! **Cobalt** 9 ins (large size) 'Gilpin & Co., Newcastle on Tyne', hamilton, £200-£300. 6oz **amber** Blackpool tower pictorial codd, only 3 examples recorded, £500-£700+. Very **dark green** Bagley & Co made 'Scarboro & Whitby' 6oz codd £150+. *BBR Auctions.*

Right; - deep blue cottage ink, extremely rare. This very fine example sold in July 1990 for £500. Price depends solely on the depth of the blue.

Above;- attractive Nailsea type speckled-body bottle with 6 applied rigaree strips, c1820-30, £250-£400.

Above;- rarely do significatnt early sealed wines of this ilk come on to the open bottle market. This important c.1670 -1680 Turks Head (London) bottle was amongst the Bob Metselaar collection sold by BBR in 1992. It realised £4,600.

Below;- a range of mostly gin bottles. The front left hand item is an embossed example depicting a figure drinking 'Cosmopoliet' £150-£200. The rear large sized bottles are particularly hard to find, £250-£300+, and the unusual handled decanter far right is an unrecorded, quite late, form £150-£200.

Main photo;- the worlds largest pot lid, **18ins diameter,** produced for an exhibition promotion and sold for "£20 each, containing 300 pots" *(presumably given free with the lid!)*. The value of such an item is extremely difficult to estimate - despite damage it is the **only recorded example.** *National Bottle Museum collection, S Yorkshire.*
Inset;- red print Scottish 'Nursery Pomade' pot lid sold in the famous Lachie Bain Sale of 1994 for £62.

Left;- labelled bottles do not surviv[e] well when buried - consequently the[y] are relatively scarce.

Beware of old pots with recentl[y] attached labels!

These three marmalade pots ar[e] original, however. Value £15 to £2[5] each, according to attractiveness[,] colour or pictorial qualities of the label[.]

Above;- two of Scotlands finest and most sought after ginger beers, both Buchan made. L to R - American Apothecaries, eagle t.m. £250 to £300+. Blue print Sang & Co, Elgin, £250-£300+.

Above;- rare **red print** Dodds Wine & Spirit Merchant, Nth & Sth Shields & Tynemouth, £75-£100.

Right;- there are times when bottle collectors can be accused of being somewhat blinkered and only chasing the popular collecting areas. Most of these night lights for example are amongst the most common type found, and yet when a large grouping are displayed back lit like this they are truly magnificent. Most are available at £5-£10 each.

Left;- one of the most striking of the figural night lights is the 'classic' head of Queen Victoria. There are other colours found but this deep blue one is highly desirable - £200+.

Above;- coloured glass fire extinguishers of the Victorian period have survived in great numbers no doubt due to their fragility. The regular cob Hardens Star costs £30-£40, the green example (far right) is much rarer - £1 to £200, as is the stunning cobalt Kalamazoo (second from right) £175 to £200 *National Bottle Museum collection, S Yorkshire.*

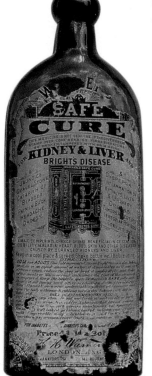

Above;- an amazing range of miniature, Compound, half pint and two pi Warners Cures vividly illustrating the glories of tsubtle colour variation The exceedingly rare green Pressburg pint (3rd from right) is valued £750-£1,000. *BBR Auctions.*

Left;- labelled English Warners are rare. This example, discovered in Scottsh cellar, sold for £40 in April 1994.

Above;- Enfield Dairy, Crumlin Rd, a scarce churn shaped pictorial cream pot with detailed and elaborate transfer £150-£200.

Above;- the worlds most expensive butter crock! The Lothian Dairy, with lid, sold for £1,900 in the Lachie Bain sale on 30th April 1994. Another example, chipped and minus lid, later sold for £1,500.

Above;- strong **blue transferred** Andrew Cameron, Ayr & Prestwick pot sold, £150-£200, though dependant upon transfer strength.

Above;- 4.75 ins tall Saltburn Creamery, J Turnbull, Saltburn & Redcar, **sepia transfer**, highly detailed print £250-£300.

Above;- trio of Doulton Lambeth water filters. The large example being particularly unusual. Value is £250-£400 depending on completeness - usually inners are missing.

Left;- unique slab seal flask D M TAGGART, VETERINARY SURGEON, HALIFAX, £500+. *BBR Auctions.*

Below;- one of the most imaginative of back lit displays - done in a collectors cellar using translucent plastic sheet stretched over a wooden frame - all in front of strip-lights. Connoisseurs will spot a fine grouping of Handysides and other quack cures here, plus a good range of inks.

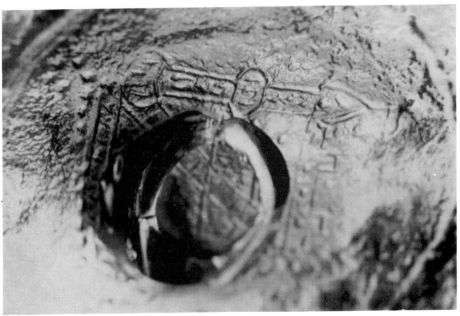

Above details of the crudely formed lip and broken pontil ring on the base which is over 2″ in diameter.

MEDICAL

"Classic" chemists bottles - contrasting shapes, colours and designs. L. to R: Emerald green, "Manx Shrub" "Fishers Seaweed Extract" - £75-£100; Red/amber "Radams Microbe Killer" - £80-£120; Cobalt blue "Prices Patent Candle Co." - £70-£80+; Aqua, "True Dafyr's Elixir" (broken pontil) - £80-£120; Large pale blue "Prices Patent Candle Co." - £150-£200+.

FIG. 1. GREAT BRITAIN.

2. THE PRINCE OF WALES.

3. SCOTLAND.

4. IRELAND.

MEDICAL

1. Robt., Turlington, Balsam of Life, clear £30-£50.
2. Roch's Embrocation, Whooping Cough, clear. £1.
3. Sir. J. Murray's Patent Recarbonated Fluid Magnesia, aqua £2.
4. Anthony's Compound Syrup of Wild Cherry, aqua. 50p.
5. Anderson Gratton's Embrocation, ice blue. £2.
6. Pecktake's For Coughs and Bronchitis, ice blue. £5.
7. G. Dutton and Son, Chest and Lung mixture, aqua. £1.
8. Veno's Seaweed Tonic, aqua. £1.
9. De Carle's Lungene, aqua. £1.
10. G. Groupline Cough Syrup, aqua. £1.
11. Mrs. Winslow's Soothing Syrup. £1.
12. Beetham's Glycerine and Cucumber, clear. £1.
13. Clarke's World Famed Blood Mixture, blue. £10-£15+.
14. Clarke's World Famed Blood Mixture, blue, 12". £20+.
15. Bishop's Granular Effervescent Piperazine blue. £2.
16. Collin's Cough Elixir. £2.
17. Talbot's Balsamic Elixir. £2.
18. Crosby's Balsamic Elixir. £2.
19. Dr. Rooke's Solar, Elixir. Blue £10+.
20. Dr. Rooke's Rheumatic Lixile, cobalt blue. £10+.
21. Congreave's Balsamic Elixir. £1.
22. Daffy's Elixir, clear. £40+.
23. Roche's Embrocation Whooping Cough, clear. £5.
24. Bishop's Hair Restorer, cobalt blue. £7-£10.
25. Mexican Hair Renewer, cobalt blue. £7-£10+.
26. Mrs. S. A. Allen's, World's Hair Restorer, London, amber. £2+.
27. Tricopherous for the Skin and Hair, aqua. £2.
28. Tricopherous for the Skin and Hair, blue. £10.
29. Madame Girrards, Hygienic Hair Restorer, amber. £10+.
30. Lockyers Sulphur Hair Restorer, aqua. £1.
31. Koko For The Hair, aqua. £1.
32. Harlene For The Hair, aqua. £1.
33. Silkodono For The Hair and Scalp, milk glass. £5.
34. Hagon's Cleanser For Children's Hair, aqua. £1.
35. Argonsair For The Children's Hair. £2.
36. Astol Hair Colour, Edwards Harlene Co., amber. £3-£5.
37. Lavona Hair Tonic, clear. £1.
38. Dr. Adolf Hommel's Haemotogen, aqua. £2-£3.
39. Dr. Wilson's Hair Restorer, aqua. £3.
40. Butterill's Hair Restorer, cobalt blue. £12-£15+.
41. Castor Oil, cobalt blue, 3" to 12". £5-£10+.
42. Odol Tooth Powder, milkglass. £2-£5.
43. Tuska, milkglass. £10-£15+.

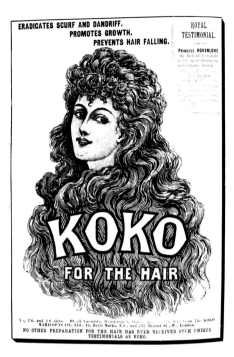

The range of 'hair' bottles known is now quite extensive and can in itself form a complete collecting category – lends itself to display in a hair dressers shop window? (especially the blue and amber glass types).

Prices remain low and for under £10 it is possible to acquire fairly rare, even one only known examples.

Shown left and below are advertisements, for two of the best known, most frequently 'dug' hair bottles.

THE MEXICAN HAIR RENEWER

Will positively restore, in every case, grey or white hair to its original colour without leaving the disagreeable smell of most "Restorers." It makes the hair charmingly beautiful, as well as promotes the growth of the hair on bald spots where the glands are not decayed.

THE MEXICAN HAIR RENEWER.

This preparation has never been known to fail in restoring the hair to its natural colour and gloss in from eight to twelve days.

It promotes growth, and prevents the hair falling out, eradicates dandruff, and leaving the scalp in a clean, healthy condition.

THE MEXICAN HAIR RENEWER

Is put up with directions in German, French, and Spanish. Retail everywhere in the kingdom at 3s. 6d. Only one size.—Sold wholesale by the ANGLO-AMERICAN DRUG COMPANY, Limited, 33, Farringdon Road, London.

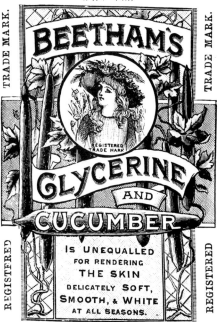

Meat Paste Pots

CROSSE & BLACKWELL

PROVISION FACTORY

Far be it for us to select an area and say here is one ripe for interest – but the highly poignant transfer printed meat paste pots must surely be such a dormant area in bottle collecting? When you consider that they are both relatively cheap to buy and yet so highly decorative, often having a coloured brown or blue transfer, as well as reflecting an early packaged past, before paper labels became the norm'.

Some folk even stick little cacti in 'em (at this point some collectors will cringe?) and thereby manage to mingle some bottles amongst the general household wares, which can have a knock-on effect by interesting casual visitors.

For how long will these pieces remain so cheap and available, especially when the full breadth of their range becomes better known?

1. **'Snelling's Potted Beef**, Rampant House St., Norwich'. Highly elaborate blue willow pattern type. £30-£50+.
2. **'G. W. Plumtree**, Railway St., Southport'. £3-£5.
3. **'Tebbutt & Cos.**, Melton Mowbray', coat of arms pic. Qualtiy pottery. £15-£20.
4. **'R. Seger**, Ipswich'. Coat of arms. £10+.

5. **'E. George**, Norwich'. £3-£5.
6. **'Robertson's**, Norwich'. £3-£5.
7. **'Oldhams**, patent digester potted beef, East Dereham'. £5+.
8. **'C. H. Berry's**, Norwich'. £3-£5.
9. **'C. Langfords**, Norwich'. £3-£5.
10. **'F. Cramptons**, Southport', sepia print transfer. £5+.

Three contrasting pots. Top; blue willow pattern 'Snellings', very rare and difficult to find in good condition. Bottom left; The 'G. W. Plumtree, Southport' pot is one of the easiest to find, and usually offers a fine transfer to boot. Right; A more quality piece of pottery is the 'Tebbutt & Cos., Melton Mowbray' pot, and a difficult one to acquire.

This late Victorian outing for men shows a bulb-neck codd bottle in everyday use.

photographs by courtesy of Peter Douglas

mineral waters

The manufacture of mineral waters (artificially celebrated drinks etc.) first began 1792 the Swiss Jacobs Schweppe in Bristol. By the mid 1800's manufacturers were widespread culminating in the 1880's when mineral waters were being produced in every small town and some villages.

The earliest bottles are the Hamilton's (also known as "torpedoes", "egg-shaped", "bowlers" etc.) whose shape when stored on their sides had the advantage that the cork remained moist and so kept the bottles air tight. (Note: Hamilton's patents was granted in 1809, referred to his method of preparing soda water not the shape of the bottle). These appeared in the early 1800's and were made in glass and stoneware. Early patents for 'uptight' bottles started in 1864 with Johnson's internal stopper quickly followed others patenting all types of internal stoppers.

Hiram Codd first patented his famous 'pop' bottle in 1870 and with subsequent patents developed his "globe-stoppered" bottle which was exported to Europe and all over the empire. This is the origins of todays Collector's "Codd" bottles.

During the next decade hundreds of different variations of this bottle and other internal stoppered bottles were patented.

Other major developments in mineral water bottle closures were: the internal screw 1871, the swing stopper 1875, the crown cork 1892.

Codd bottles were used up until the 1940's in Britain and are still manufactured and used in India today!

Mineral waters are one of the most popular branches of bottle collecting as their wide variety of contrasting shapes and colours and history can make very exciting displays.

The cobalt blue bottle is still the most sought after closely followed by the black glass variety (even rarer!).

The early Hamiltons in glass or stoneware are always going to be rare and will always command a good price.

Coloured patent mineral water bottles will also always be in demand because of their aesthetic qualities.

A superb example of an early salt-glazed Hamilton incised: "G M Hopkins, St. Ives" (c. 1850). £250+.

MINERAL WATERS

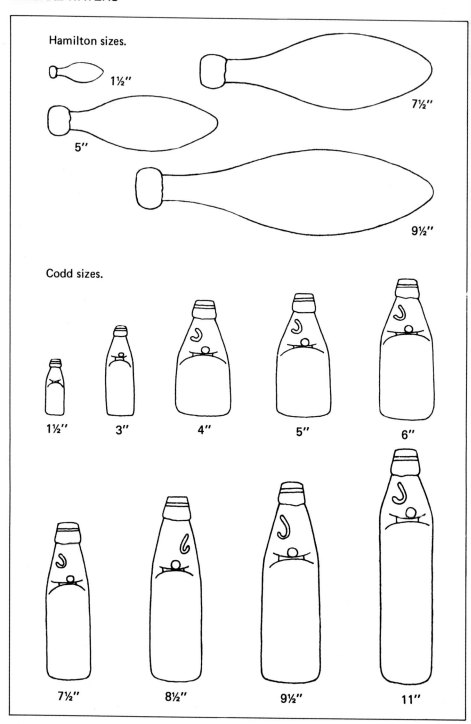

Hamilton sizes.

1½"

5"

7½"

9½"

Codd sizes.

1½"   3"   4"   5"   6"

7½"   8½"   9½"   11"

H1. Hamilton, embossed, aqua. £2-£5+.
H2. Hamilton, pictorially embossed, aqua. £5-£10+.
H3. Hamilton, embossed, clear. £30-£50.
H4. Hamilton, embossed, brown. £100-£150+.
H5. Hamilton, embossed, olive. £30-£50.
H6. Hamilton, embossed, green. £100-£200+.
H7. Hamilton, embossed, blue. £100-£500+.
H8. Hamilton, embossed, black. £200+.
H9. Hamilton, embossed, broken pontil. £500-£1000.
H10. Hamilton, aqua, 1 1/2". £25-£30+.
H11. Hamilton, aqua, 5". £20-£30.
H12. Hamilton, screw-top, aqua. £100+.

S1. Seltzer, dumpy, amber. £5-£10+.
S2. Seltzer, dumpy, green. £5-£10+.
S3. Seltzer, dumpy, aqua. £3-£10+.
S4. Seltzer, dumpy, round bottom, amber. £20-£30+.
S5. Carlsburga, seltzer, spherical, amber. £40-£50+.

Ginger beer, aqua. £3-£5.
Ginger beer, amber. £7-£10+.
Ginger beer, green. £8-£12+.
Ginger beer, black. £5-£10.

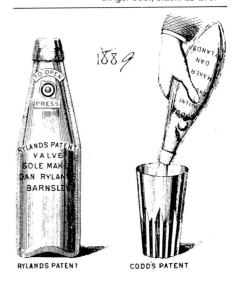

RYLANDS PATENT   CODD'S PATENT

Round bottom cylinder, aqua. £2-£20.
Round bottom cylinder, amber. £30-£50.
Round bottom cylinder, green. £40-£50.
Round bottom cylinder, blue. £50-£100+.

Mineral water, cork top, aqua. £1-£2.
Mineral water, cork-top (green, amber or brown). £2-£5.
Mineral water, screw-top (green, amber or brown). £1-£2+.
Mineral water, crown-top (green, amber or brown). 50p-£2.

by courtesy of "Codds Wallop"

Codd variations: (l-r) Reliance 'W and G Roseveare, Barnsley', £5-£10, Circular 'bulb' neck 'John Adams, Jersey' £5-£10+, 'bulb' neck 'Jordan and Addington, St. Neots' £2-£5, 6 oz emerald Dobson's patent 'Wadsworth, Cambridge' £250+, Beavis shape 'Thomas and Evans, Porth' £5-£10, Haynes patent 'Mayo and Rugg, Earlsdon, Coventry' £100-£150.

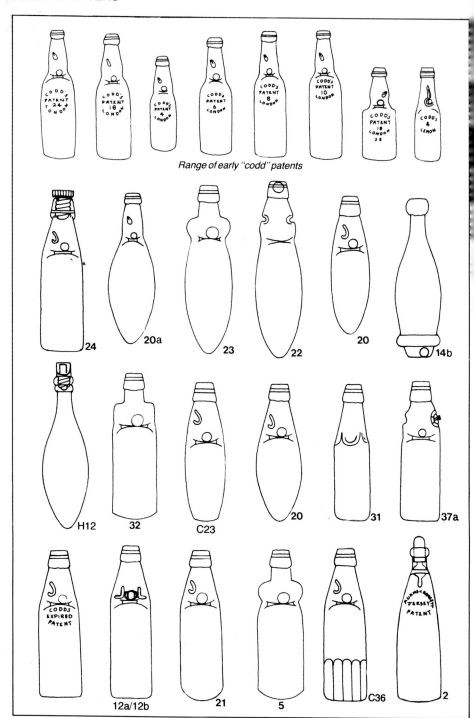

Range of early "codd" patents

C1.   Codd, embossed, aqua. £1-£5.
C2.   Codd, pictorially embossed, aqua. £2-£5+.
C3.   Codd, embossed, clear. £20-£30+.
C4.   Codd, embossed, amber. £20-£30+.
C5.   Codd, embossed, brown. £30-£50+.
C6.   Codd, embossed, olive. £50-£100+.
C7.   Codd, embossed, green. £70-£100+.
C8.   Codd, embossed, blue. £750-£1000+.
C9.   Codd, blue lip, aqua. £30-£100+.
C10. Codd, green lip, aqua. £75-£150+.
C11. Codd, amber lip, aqua. £50-£100+.
C12. Codd, blue marble, aqua. £20-£30.
C13. Codd, green marble, aqua. £20-£30.
C14. Codd, amber marble, aqua. £20-£30.
C15. Codd, early shape, aqua. £20-£30+.
C16. Codd's 4 Lemon, aqua. £20+.
C17. Codd, early shape, amber. £200-£500+.
C18. Codd, early shape, green. £300-£500+.

C22. Codd, early shape, dumpy, amber, 5 1/2". £500+.
C23. Skittle Codd, aqua. £50-£100.
C24. Skittle Codd, blue. £1000+.
C25. Codd, aqua, medicine, no marble, 1 1/2". £50-£75.
C26. Codd, aqua 3". £100-£200.
C27. Codd, dumpy, aqua, 4". £150-£200+.
C28. Codd, dumpy, aqua, 5". £100-£200+.
C29. Codd, dumpy, aqua, 7". £50+.
C30. Codd, dumpy, amber, 4". £500+.
C31. Codd, dumpy, green, 5". £500+.
C32. Codd, early shape, green, 5 1/2". £300-£500+.
C33. Codd, large, aqua, 10". £10-£15+.
C34. Codd, tall, aqua, 11". £10-£15+.
C35. Codd, display, aqua, 3'. £200+.
(Note: the mould for this bottle is in the United Glass Ltd.'s museum. We have never seen one but they were made!!)
C36. Codd, fluted base, aqua. £10+.
C37. Codd, octagonal base, aqua. £10+.
C38. Codd, octagonal base, amber. £100+.
C39. Codd, octagonal sides, aqua. £50-£100.
C40. Codd, round bottom, aqua. £50-£100.

Left to right: Aqua octagonal codd - £50-£100; aqua octagonal base codd - £10+; amber octagonal base codd - £100+; aqua octagonal codd - £30-£50.

MINERAL WATERS

1. **Acme** Patent, codd, aqua. £2-£5+.
2. **Adams and Barrett** Patent, long wood stopper, aqua. £30.
3. **Barrett and Eler's** Patent, long wood stopper, aqua. £20-£30+.
3a. **Barrett and Eler's** Patent, long wood stopper, aqua (small size). £30-£50+.
4. **Beavis** Patent, codd, aqua. £5-£10.
5. **Bulb-top**, Dumpy codd, aqua. £2+.
6. **Caley's** Patent Codd. £150-£200.
7. **Chapman's Patent**, rubber ball, internal stopper, aqua. £10-£20.
7a. **Chapman's Patent**, rubber ball, four dimples in shoulder, aqua. £20-£30+.
8. **Chapman's**, internal metal stopper, aqua. £20.
9. **Connor's** Patent, oval marble, aqua. £80-£120+.
10. **Connor's** Patent, pear shaped marble. £80-£120+.
11. **Deek's** Patent, codd, aqua. £50-£75.
12. **Dobsons** Patent, 4-way wood or glass stopper. £5.
13. **Eclipse** Patent, shouldered codd with small dimples on sides. £30-£50.
14. **Edward's** Patent, internal stopper, aqua. £15-£20.s
14a. **Edward's** Patent with wired on conversion for corked bottles. £50-£75+.
14b. Edward's Patent, marble, ring round base, aqua. £150-£200+.
14c. Edward's patent, marble, ring round base, aqua. £150-£200+.
15. **Empress** Patent, codd, aqua-inclined. £15-£20.
16. **Hayne's** Patent, oval marble, aqua. £80-£100+.
17. **Hill's** Patent, codd, aqua. £50+.
18. **Horner's** Patent conversion for cork closure bottles. £50-£100.
19. **Hutchinson** Patent (American botle rarely found in U.K.). £20+.
20. **Hybrid**, aqua. £20-£50.
20a. **Hybrid**, early shape, aqua. £30-£50+.
20b. **Hybrid**, amber. £1000.
20c. **Hybrid**, coloured lip. £200-£500.
21. **Hybrid**, round bottom, aqua. £30-£50+.
22. **Reliance** Patent, hybrid, aqua. £150-£200.
23. **Hybrid**, bulb-top, aqua. £200+.
24. **Internal**, codd, screw-top, aqua. £200+.
25. **Lamont's** Patent, internal stopper, aqua. £5-£10.

25a. **Lamont's** Hybrid, wooden stopper with rubber ring. £30-£50+.
26. **Mill's** Patent, bee-hive lip, aqua. £10-£15+.
27. **Mitchell's** Patent, 2 shoulder levels, glass stopper. £150-£200.
28. **Niagra** bottle 4-lugged codd. £2+.
29. **Nuttall's** Patent, codd, aqua. £5.
30. **Ormond's** Patent, wooden stopper. £200-£250.
31. **Codd's Premier** Patent, glass marble, amber. £20-£30+.
31a. **Codd's Premier** Patent, glass marble, amber. £200+.
32. **Reliance** Patent, codd, aqua. £2-£5.
33. **Shaw's** Patent, codd, aqua. £5-£10.
33a. **Shaw's** Patent, "Roseveares" variant horizontal ribs. £5-£10.
34. **Sutclife's** Patent, recess round middle, intenal stopper, aqua. £150-£200+.
34a. **Sutcliffe's** Patent, scallopped shoulder, internal stopper, aqua. £15-£20.
34b. **Sutcliffe's** Patent, internal stopper, aqua. £5.
35. **Syke's Mackvay** patent, six dimples in base, internal stopper, aqua. £30-£50.
35a. **Syke's Mackvay**, early type, no dimples. £20-£30+.
36. **Vallet's** patent, interⁿ.ₐᵣ stopper, aqua. £5.
37. **Valve** Codd, without retaining lug. £75-£100.
37a. **Valve** codd by Rylands. £50-£75+.

"Snowdrop" fluted internal Stopper £10
Ridged internal stopper £8
"Globe" amber internal stopper £25

119

MINERAL WATERS

LITHIA WITH CITRATE OF POTASH, 3s. 6d.
BROMIDE OF POTASH WATER, 3s. 6d.
CITRATE OF POTASH WATER, 2s. 6d.
CITRATE OF POTASH WITH IRON, 3s.
POTASH, 2s. 6d. SODA, 2s.
LEMONADE, etc., 2s. 6d.
Orders for twelve dozen carriage free.
HOGG, 9, Albion Place, Hyde Park Square.

← Range of normal codd sizes:

Above opposite: Centre: Standard Hamilton "Hooper and Co. Chemists to H M Queen, Royal German Spa and Pall Mall E." £12-£15.
Top: Left - "Maughan's Patent Carra Water" - £30-£50; Centre - Hamilton stand £20-£30; Left - 'Cucumber' - "John Hill, Irby Nr. Spilsby" - £10-£15.
Front: Left - Crown Closure "Wilners Aerated Waters, Newport Pagnell" - £5; Right - short 'Cucumber' "James Burgess, Luton, Beds." £5-£10.

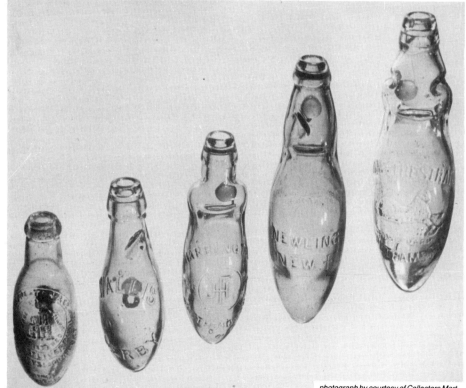

photograph by courtesy of Collectors Mart

Left to right: Split-size wooden bullet stopper "W. Preston and Co., 2A, Gill Street, Liverpool" and "Stanley Street, Southport" - £50-£100 (made by Nuttall and Co. St. Helens; "Wallis-Derby" - (2 only known) 6 oz. size, no cross-pinch in neck - £300+; 6 oz. Bulb neck Hybrid "Harrington Southend-on-Sea (Sykes Mackvay, Castleford) - £200+; 10 oz. Hybrid, "Newling, Newcross" (Barrett and Foster, London) - £50+; 10 oz. "Dan Ryland's Reliance Patent" (1885), "Hine and Trestral, Southampton" (Rylands, Barnsley) - £150-£200.

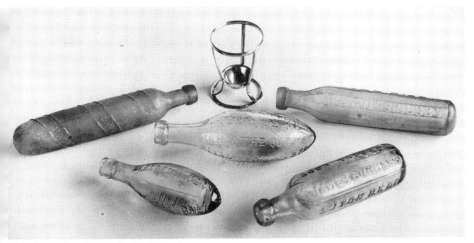

Photo by courtesy "Mainly Codd's Wallop"

Advertisement in "The Mineral Water Maker's Manual Diary for 1895".

MINERAL WATERS

photograph by courtesy of "Codd's Wallop"

Selection of Mineral Water Bottle shapes:- (L to R) Upright cylindrical blob top "Rawlings": Long neck, dumpy bodied type "Wm. Brown, the Crystal Aerated Water Works, Ferrybridge"; Cylindrical, with "chisel" stopper "James Cox, Bethnal Green Rd"; Standard "reputed" pint type with int. screw stopper "Trask's Carbonated Beverages - prepared with filtered water, Yeovil"; Standard half pint, with int. screw thread - honeyamber "R. White's 1/4d. deposit charged"; Flat bottomed Hamilton, machine made, blob top Schweppes - as supplied to the King and Prince of Wales"; Applied lip, Crown "Kirby and McKee, Bletchley".

Rare coloured contrasting codd bottles, L. to R.:- emerald green, early shape, 1/2 size, dumpy codd "RICHARDSON, HARROGATE" - £500-£750; bulb-top, amber codd "Goffe & Sons" - "Birmingham" - £500+; cobalt blue, Dodd's patent codd - £500+.

A codd bottle being made by hand. The craftsman is putting the finishing touches to the "applied" lip after the marble (stopper) has been placed in the neck of the bottle.

Collectors with their old "Pop" Bottles.
(Mineral water bottle Collectors)

Tim Wood, Warrington, holding rare amber codd embossed 'Groves & Whitnall', with pict. of arm holding arrow, 1982.

Diana Snowden holding a round bottomed hybrid, 1982.

Dunfermline digger Eddy Berry holding Scotland's only codd. 'Scottish Co-op Wholesale Society'.

Only recorded 'Wakefield Patent' dug in the Merseyside area in 1981.

Roy Hambleton, Leek, digger of a time valve codd, with basal retaining jugs.

Denis & Graham from Manchester with a unique patent they dug in 1983.

Mick Hunnam holding cobalt 'Bradford Bros., Newcastle', flat bottom hamilton, 1983.

BARNETT & FOSTER,

Mineral Water and Ice Machinists, Bottle and Box Makers, Manufacturing Chemists, and
GENERAL PROVIDERS FOR THE AERATED WATER, WINE, BEER, AND CYDER TRADES.

3 Gold, 2 Silver, and 2 Bronze Medals, International Health Exhibition, London, 1884. Latest—
5 Highest Awards, Adelaide, 1887. 2 Highest Awards, Newcastle-on-Tyne, 1887.

Opposite; some weird and rare codds. Top row, Diana Snowden, Notts. activist, holding a round bottomed hybrid at the 1982 Winternational. Tim Wood, Warrington, proudly holding a rare amber 'Groves & Whitnall' codd with pictorial of arm holding an arrow, which he dug in 1982. Centre row, Eddy Berry, Dunfermline, with Scotland's only black codd, 'Scottish Co-operative Wholesale Society', that he dug. Roy Hambleton, from Leek, with the valve he dug, with basal retaining lugs. Right, the only recorded 'Wakefield Patent', found in the Merseyside area in 1981. Bottom row, Dennis & Graham, two lucky diggers from Manchester, with a unique and remarkable patent they found in 1983. Mick Hunnam with his cobalt flat bottomed crown capped hamilton 'Bradford Bros., Newcastle'.

Miniatures

Top row: "Martell Brandy", labelled - £2, amber "Sauce" - £5, aqua "Lady's Leg" neck liqueur - £3-£5, aqua "Coffee" sample - £1, shear-lip "H.P." Sauce - £5, black glass liqueur - £30-£50, Bottom row: Black glass Benedictine - £2+, dark green "Gordon's gin" - £2+, aqua "O.T" Cordial - £3-£5, aqua "Manor Blood Food" - £5-£10, aqua "Idris" Cordial - £3-£5, aqua "Rose's" Lime Juice - £3-£5.

L to R: Transferred 'Normal' extract pot; a blue topped miniature Doulton water jug (featuring the obligatory hunting scenes); cobalt sheared-lip 'J. Lewis, London' hamilton shape originally used for perfume; two-tone transferred 'Ivanhoe' whisky jug (almost 2½″ high); salt glazed G.B. transferred 'Stiff & Sons, Lambeth'.

Back row, L to R: Mini sealed gin with rolled lip; milkglass Hartwig Kantorowicz gin; Lucas Bols sealed wine; black glass Roses Lime Juice. Middle row, L to R: Doulton water jugs; transferred Fields Ink; Nirvana codd shape; beer bottle shaped perfume with label; Udolpho Wolfes Schnapps; transferred flagon. Third row, L to R: Transfereed Normal Co. jar; two-tone transferred Mercury jar; Bourne & Sons g.b.; Hull g.b.; Radams Microbe Killer with blue writing, and a gosnell pot lid leaning up against it. Front row: Five different mini-miniature g.b.s.

This Miniature Bottle Collection entitled the "Village Shop" was exhibited at various bottle shows in England and won many prizes for the proud owners Glyn & Cathie Gilbert.

Top Row:

1. "RADAM'S MICROBE KILLER - LONDON" miniature flagon with incised blue print. £100-£150.
2. "Odol Tooth Powder" milk glass flask. £10+.
3. Ginger Beer two-tone honey top: blue transfer 'Warrington Lane, J. Fairhurst, Wigan,' incised on back: "Bourne Denby". £50-£75.
4. Miniature Ginger Beer, saltglazed, incised on shoulder: "J. Stiff & Sons, Lambeth". £100-£200.
5. Ginger Beer two-tone with honey top: black transfer "Bourne and Denby". £50-£100.
6. Miniature Pot Lid "carbolic Tooth Paste, Calverts, 6d, 1/- and 1/6". £30-£50.
7. Miniature Pot Lid "Cherry Tooth Paste, John Gosnell, Free Sample". £40-£60.
8. Pot Lid, lip salve, gold print of ladies head on pink background. £50+.
9. Perfume or Whisky flagon, two tone brown top, salt glazed, incised on base "Doulton, Lambeth, England". £20-£30.
10. Miniature Perfume "J. Lewis, London, "blue shear lip hamilton. £150-£200+.

11. Bellarmine Jug, brown top, slip-glaze, incised on base: "Doulton, Lambeth, England". £100+.

Bottom Row:

1. "Lime Juice, Rose & Co., black glass. £40-£50.
2. "Scotch Whisky Camble, Hope and King" flagon, white with buff top, pottery mark. "Price & Sons". £3-£5.
3. Dark green glass miniature liquer bottle - Benedictine. £2+.
4. Sample two-tone Honey top Flagon, black transfer "Price Sons and Company, Stoneware Manufacturers, Bristol". £50+.
5. Square Flagon two-tone, incised base "Doulton, Lambeth, England". £40-£50+.
6. "Khoosh Bitters", amber glass. £20-£30.
7. Salt-glazed bottle incised, "Oute Gerever, Prosit, S. Van Dujkazin, Amsterdam". £10+.
8. Aqua square Zara liqueur with glass seal on side. £40-£50+.

Door in centre.

9. Top row; miniature sample ginger beers. £10-£20+.
10. Bottom row; miniature sample blacking jars. £10-£15+.

Left to right; aqua, shear lip H.P. sauce - £5; Ladies leg, aqua, liqueur - £3-£5, Milk glass, 'codd' - £5, Miniature sample, salt glazed G.B., incised "Bourne, Denby" - £30-£40+, blue top, flagon, "Dairy Supply Co. Ltd., £25-£30+. Buff top, whisky, "A Wee Tootie" - £5+.

Group of common miniature bottles (apart from "Dairy Supply" flagon and "Roderick John", whisky flagon) all of which can be bought for a few pounds or less.

Ointment Pots

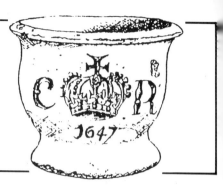

Most ointment pots are quite small in size and the transferred Victorian varieties, which we are the most interested in, often hold quaint and extraordinary wild claims and statements in keeping with the general quack practices of the period.

It is the small size and wild claims which undoubtedly make them so popular with bottle collectors, indeed prices for these particular items have risen more dramatically than any other category since publication of our 1983 Price Guide.

The word ointment stems from the latin 'unguentum'. The early Greeks were fond of exercise, followed by a bath, and would then anoint themselves with perfumed oils.

From Elizabethan times ointment pots and pill pots were made, though rarely are the early pieces decorated. In fact, plain Delftware pots from the second half of the 17th century, in simple tin glazed enamel, are now quite scarce.

Two different sizes of Dutch delft pots, type 3. Hand thrown and subtly coloured. £30-£50.

This cabinet of ointment pots, belonging to Dr. Anne Young, may well have sparked off the increased interest in this area since 1983? Of particular importance is the 'Delescot' Delft pot on the bottom shelf. Such rare items as this command £250+ when they appear in auction rooms.

Two sides of type 15, blue transfer, £7 to £10+. This is always a very crudely transferred pot, often smudged, indicating slightly earlier manufacture than most of the others found.

1. **Amol skin food,** Cardiff, head pic., overglaze pot, 2 1/4 ins. £10-£15.
2. **Cleopatra complexion cream,** York, head pict., overglaze pot, 2 1/4 ins. £10-£15.
3. **Dutch delft,** tin glazed pot, hand thrown, various sizes and subtle colour variations, rarely mint. £30-£50.
4. **Dr. Rookes golden ointment,** C Rooke, M.D., Scarborough, phoenix t.m. £100-£150+.
5. **Dr. Rookes golden ointment,** as above but without the pict., t.m. £50+.
6. **Dr. Wilsons eczema cure,** no place name, very varied lettering, 1 3/4 ins. £50-£75.
7. **Egyptian Salve,** Reade Bros & Co. Ltd., Wolverhampton, 1 1/2 ins. £10+.
8. **Friend in need ointment,** Dudley, wide mouth transferred all round, 1 1/4 ins. £30-£50.
9. **Holloways ointment,** 113 Southwark Street, London, several variations, 1 3/4 ins. £10+.
10. **Izal ointment,** Newton Chambers, Sheffield, turquoise transfer both sides, 2 1/2 ins. £15-£20+.
11. **Lees ointment,** 4, 5 & 6 Smithfields Street, Paisley. Stanley Castle, t.m., brown. £150-£200.
12. **Moonseed ointment,** the great household remedy, Swindon, 2 ins. £50+.
13. **Morses herbal ointment,** 10, 11 & 12 Regent St., Swindon, Wilts., 1 3/4 ins. £50+.
14. **Natures herbal ointment,** straight sided tall pot, lots writing, several sizes. £10-£15.
15. **Poor Mans Friend,** Beach & Barnicott, blue all round transfer, 1 1/2 ins. £7-£10+.
16. **Randall's celebrated ointment,** Plymouth, wide, printed all round, 1 1/2 ins. £30+.
17. **Singletons eye ointment,** shallow pot with finger-hold pedestal, blue print. £2-£3+.
18. **Star carbolic ointment,** sepia transfer, tall pot. £150-£200.
19. **The ointment,** prepared by G. Handyside, very plain but extremely rare, 1 1/2 ins. £100+.
20. **The ointment,** D. J. McKinnon, Dundee, large 3 ins., tall pot. £75-£100+.

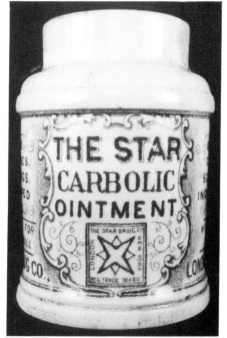

Type 18 featuring a sepia transfer, £150 - £200+. Amongst the more sought after of ointments.. 'London, New York'... wonder if any have turned up in America?

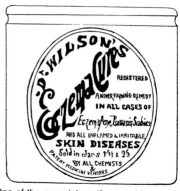

One of the more interesting graphic lay-outs is this Dr. Wilsons Eczema Cure, which combines considerable variation of letter styles. Type 6 - £50-£75..

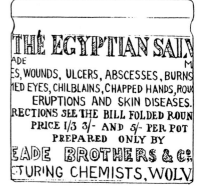

A simple but effective Egyptian Salve pot giving a list of the different sizes available. This, type 7, is the 1/3d size, 3d for tax. The larger expensive ones employed a pot lid with base. £10+.

An earlier pot than the Egyptian Salve, given away by the lower 1 1/2d tax? This is a variant to type 9 - £10+. This ointment extends to five further sizes, which employ the famous 'seated lady' pictorial pot lid (see pot lids section).

Above; the three stages in the development toward the now fairly common Singletons Eye Ointment, of unusual shape. Top piece, about end of 18th century, is finely thrown compared to the later bulkier shape. These are complete, the top having held just a sixteenth of an inch of the precious ointment. The story of the Singletons empire from the late 1700's to 1949 is highly eventful, including, along the way, the potter Stephen Green. He married into the family and aided the prosperity with his skills. The lower of the three, type 17, is by far the easiest ointment to discover, though early variations are possible to stumble on with luck, and with a swift eye!

Possibly the 'daddy' of them all. This is the Isola Bishops Balm pot lid - the same attractive pictorial is featured on maybe the rarest and most sought after of UK ointment pots. £350-£300+.

POISONS

In terms of Shows 1985 was the year of the first U.K. National, in bottle terms it was undoubtedly the year of the poison. However the two combined when Brian Thatchers stunning display of poisons at the National walked off with the overall 'Best of Show' award.

The hobby has seen many leaps and bounds in prices, trends come and go etc., but the increase in poison prices during the last 12 months has staggered everyone.

This is not so hard to understand. The vibrant blues and greens, to ward off accidental day-time consumption, and the uniquely shaped patent types, to ware off accidental consumption at night (when lighting the gas lamp was fiddly), all display so magnificently – as Brian Thatcher sowed us all!

Roy Morgan's book 'Benign Blue' coffin contains a wealth of information for the poison specialist, though now sadly out-dated a little and also out of print. It has become a bible to those inspired by this category, especially the original patent specification pages.

A display of poisons with the now almost obligatory human skull incorporated.

C. H. LEE & CO.,

MANUFACTURERS OF

SKULL & CROSS BONES

(LEE POISON BOTTLE.)

117 PEARL ST., BOSTON.

Room 313, 132 Nassau St., New York.

[O. EP]

Patented June 26, 1894.

Selecting the single most outstanding and desirable bottle within the category of poisons would surely lead all to the same conclusion – the cobalt skull shape, type 21.

This somewhat bizarre item, modelled in the shape of a human skull, features the word POISON, embossed on the forehead, and displays a fine set of gnashers!

Charlton H. Lees' patent, no. 23,399, bottle is rare both in America, where it originates, and in England. About 8 have been found here – all from the North Wales/Chester area.

In America there is a blue glazed pottery reproduction, which should fool nobody, in fact it can enable collectors to add an example of this rare item to their shelves, without massive outlay of cash.

This sales card was discovered in a chemist's shop in Rhyl, North Wales during the demolition of buildings, together with 2 sets of cobalt blue skull poisons, in 1982. Before this date this American bottle was never known to have been sold in England chemists' shops.

POISONS

Above, a rare complete set of Admiralty poisons, type 1, complete with ground glass stoppers. All recovered from a single Scottish dump by one lucky digger.

Above L. to R.; type 2, one of the Inmans variations, type 4, type 5.

1. **Admiralty.** Square, cobalt, ground glass stopper. 16 oz (7 1/2 ins tall), 8 oz, 4 oz & 2 oz capacities (latter the rarest). Front panel incorportates War Dept. broad arrow and letter 'N8'. £20-£100.

2. **Ammonia, Inmans.** Tall stoneware with brown neck, transfer features eagle and list of stores. Several variations. £30-£50+.

3. **Ammonia, Jumbomonia.** Large transferred stoneware which doubles as a hot water bottle after contents are gone. £150-£200.

4. **Ammonia, Sharps.** Green glass, triangular. Embossed 'Sharps Ammonia, Glasgow, Poisonous, Not To Be Taken'. £30-£50.

5. **Ammonia, Yapoo.** Oval, front covered in raised bumps. Similar types with no brand name. Cobalt to mid blue. £30-£40.

6. **As previous** except dark green/black. £20-£30.

7. **As previous** except golden amber. £30-£40.

8. **Crescent,** several sizes, 5 ins. commonest. Front panel indented with herringbone pattern either side of centre. Cobalt, amber & brown. £15-£30.

9. **As previous** except light blue & green. £15-£30.

10. **Hexagonal, vertical ribbing** on 2 adjacent panels and Poison, or Poisonous, Not to Be Taken on front panel. 2 ins. up to 8 ins,. Clear, aqua, amber, green and blue. Small sizes. £2-£10.

11. **As previous** but the larger size. £10-£20.

12. **Hexagonals, irregular** sized panels, Not to be taken, down front panel, diamond protrusions or vertical ribbing either side. Sizes and colours as varied as in normal hexagons, prices accordingly broad. £2-£10.

13. **Hexagonal with burst lip.** Poisonous/Not to be taken on front panel, ribbing either side. Approx. 6 ins. tall, cobalt. £15-£20.

14. **As previous** but in aqua glass. £3-£5.

15. **Lysol.** Dumpy shape with embossed cross hatching, numerous embossing variations and several sizes. Aqua, amber, brown, light blue & green. £2-£10+.

16. **As previous** but in cobalt blue. £10-£20.

17. **Martins.** Side lying, prominet 'U' shaped neck. 'The Martin Poison Bottle' embossed on one side "Poison" on other . 2oz, 4 oz & 8 oz in aqua/light blue. £100-£200.

18. **As previous** but 16 oz size, extremely rare. £300-£500.

19. **McDougalls Arsenate of Lead.** Stone jar, off-white with crude black transfer. £50-£100.

20. **Quines,** cylindrical wedge shape, sloping up at angle. 2 oz, 4 oz and 8 oz sizes in aqua glass. £150-£200+.

Above; an uncommon and novel type 3 stoneware bottle which doubles up as a hot water bottle when the contents have been emptied.

POISONS

Above, an extremely rare Thumb-nail poison, type 24, heavily embossed in ribs and diamond shapes, and the whole shaped to snugly fit the hand.

Above, a rare type 19 with a heavy but crude black transfer upon a murky grey/cream ground and featuring a wide mouth.

Above; L. blue Lysol, type 16, alongside a rare labelled example, from the Colin Gould collection.

138

21. **Skull,** distinctive skull shape, found in 3 sizes, cobalt glass. (Reproduced in pottery also). Very rare. £500-£1000+.

22. **Star,** so called due to its star-shaped cross section. Embossed, rear, Rd. No. 716057. Green/ Olive. £40-£50+.

23. **As previous** but in cobalt blue. £50-£75+.

24. **Thumb-Nail,** cobalt, approx. 4 ins. tall. Curved back with vertical and diamond shaped embossing, front flat with impressed thumb-accomodating indent. Extremely rare. £200-£300.

25. **Warning.** Odd shaped side-lying bottle, amber. On base 'Warning Poison, Trade J.P. Mark Reg. no. 579349'. Very rare. £500-£750.

26. **Wasp Waist** (Eclipse patent). Cobalt blue. Pronounced narrow centre 'waist'. Three sizes and some variations on body embossing, with or without diamond. £1,000-£1,500.

Above L. a very rare type 25, R. type 9, front type 20.

Above L. back a type 2, R. type 26, front type 17.

Above L. the common type 10, alongside a type 12.

139

"WARNING" POISON BOTTLE.

DISTINCTIVE SHAPE.

WILL NOT STAND UP.

NO SHOULDERS OR CREVICES.

EMPTIED WITHOUT DIFFICULTY.

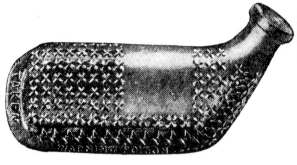

(Reg. No. 579341)

Some poisons have risen dramatically in price during the last 2 years or so. The rare ones, especially, have witnessed astronomical increases. Shown right is a type 25 'Warning' bottle. It is an attractive amber colour, with a roughly triangular body shape, and an oddly bent-over neck. The advertisement above proclaims its many virtues. This shape was patented by J. Dowell in 1912 along with a patented neck band for a wired-on stopper.

Poisonous Substances

Poisons and Pharmacy Act, 1908,

Regulations

as added to by Order in Council, March 22, 1911.

Sale not confirmed to chemists and druggists, but all persons selling these articles *by retail* must distinctly label the box, bottle, vessel, wrapper or cover with –

1. The name of the substance.

2. The word "Poisonous."

3. The Words "Not to be taken" *printed on the label.*

4. Name and address of the seller.

5. If a liquid, the bottle or container must be "rendered distinguishable by touch from ordinary bottles or containers."

One of the most remarkable black and white pot lids is this example shown above. Both the lay-out and illustration do the engraver proud, as well as showing the effective advertising appeal of the medium. £250-£300+. This range of pictorial 'Potted Meats' will be dealt with more thoroughly in Volume 2.

ROWLAND'S
ODONTO
A NON GRITTY TOOTH POWDER

Pot Lids

The story behind the evolvement of the huge range of pot lids is very much entangled with the rapid development of the industrial revolution. Certainly the increasing prosperity enabled ladies and gentlemen of the day to make full use of the cosmetic pomades, bears grease, cold creams, tooth pastes, the medically wonderous ointments, lip salves, and the new fangled sandwich spreads of bloater paste, mushroom savoury and potted game.

Indeed, by the mid nineteenth century the range of products packaged and marketed commercially in glazed pots, with their transfer printed tops, is readily apparent upon walking round any Bottle Show today. Pot lids are the 2nd most popular specialist category under the banner of bottle collecting.

Whilst multi-coloured Pratt-style lids remain, in the majority of cases, in the domain of the antiques 'clan', the more often dug monochrome pot lids are becoming much better established as both highly attractive & historically important. The better pieces have even proved remarkably sound investments too. 1985 should see the re-emergence of the hard-back 'Black & White Pot Lids' with a revised price guide. This will undoubtedly give this facet of the hobby a 'shot in the arm'.

The trickle of unrecorded specimens continued through dump digging, and bargains from Antique shops and fairs, though new collectors need to be particularly wary of fakes and reproductions which have appeared over the years. Transfers of photographs can now be easily applied to plain pot lids with a low firing glazing method – news on fakes is constantly monitored in the pages of British Bottle Review.

Above; the ever popular and attractive Jewsbury & Brown pot lid (type 28) with marbled border and base continues to hold its appeal and price, and introduces many a new collector into this facet of 'bottling'. £10-£15.

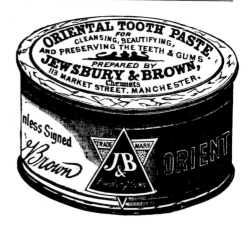

Advertisement in "Chemists and Druggists Diary 1889".

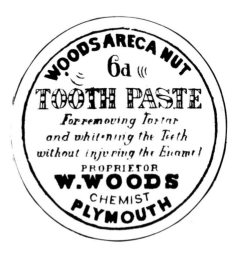

Above and right; 'The advert and the pot lid'. Type 45, Woods Areca Nut Tooth Paste 6d size, is dug up all over the world – Australia, New Zealand, South Africa, and even America where pot lids are not so profuse.

Several collectors in the Plymouth area, where Woods was based, have put together extensive collections of Woods' variations. Even the one shown right comes in a red transferred varient – £15+.

Roger Green and David Lewis wrote a book entitled 'The Advertising Art of Printed Pot Lids'. They both have Art training and were each drawn into this area of collecting for the artistic beauty many lids show. Certainly the above two bear sound testament to the great skills of the engraver of the copper or steel plate from which the transfers were taken. The sophistication and inventiveness often belies that the engravers themselves were only semi-literate.

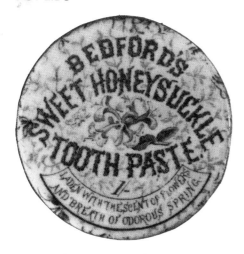

The range of colours available on monochrome pot lids extends beyond merely black and white. This page shows other colours found, top L. & R. 'Bedfords Sweet Honeysuckle Tooth Paste', both top and base in a subtle brown print. Centre L. a red print 'Ama Rosa' oval lid, type 5. Centre R. a light brown Army & Navy Almond Shaving Cream, the anchovy paste from the same firm can also be found in green print. Right the Borax pot lid has a blue transfer and base. Here is an advertisement for same.

Pictorial portrait pot lids, predominantly women, hold an especial charm and fascination for the serious collector. The above display shows twelve particularly desirable such lids.

Above left, the ubiquitous 'Kranol, unsurpassed, great hair food', type 31 - £75-£100. Very few of these have been actually dug, the majority surfaced from a Cheshire cellar just over 15 years ago. Only around 50 were found, but less than half were in mint condition. Above R., a real tongue twister 'Mrs. Ellen Hales Celebrated Heal All Ointment', type 23 - £30+. A fine pictorial but not one of the prettiest of faces depicted?

Variations upon a theme! The above three pairs of lids each bears similarity to their 'sister' in one way or another. The top two are subtle variants of the attractive 'May Roberts' girl with folded arms, only the lower line of writing distinguishes them. Centre; two stunning 'R. B. Edes, Shaving Cream', one with the man looking in the mirror the other looking away. One of these sold for £250 in 1984. Bottom pair; left, Dr Zeimers Alexandra, type 2 - £40-£75 with the woman looking to the right, next to it is the 'Sharp Bros.' look-alike - surely a clear case of copying.

Above L., type 4 - £150-£200, R. type 9 - £50+.

1. **American Dentifrice,** C.R. Coffin, Manchester. £10-£20.
2. **Alexandra** t.p., woman pictorial, Dr. Zeimers, several transfer variations. £40-£75.
3. **Alexandra** t.p., woman pictorial, Dr. Zeimers, miniature version. £150+.
4. **Alexandra,** The, Cherry t.p., Alfred Felton, Melbourne, girl pictorial, 2 coloured ground, includes diam. reg. mark. £150-£200.
5. **Ama Rosa,** t.p., oval shape, red print. £50-£75+.
6. **Army & Navy,** anchovy paste or potted meats, small central pictorial. £7-£12.
7. **Army & Navy,** as above but in green print. £12-£15.
8. **An excellent Relish,** potted beef, bloater paste, anchovy paste etc. £5-£10.
9. **Bales Mushroom Savoury,** brown print, mushroom pictorial. £50+.
10. **Bon Marche,** Liverpool, building pictorial, very rare. £250-£300

11. **Burgess's Anchovy Paste** with base, Victorian coat of arms. £5-£10.
12. **Blanchflower,** farmyard scene, Great Yarmouth. £150-£200+.
13. **Blanchflower Bloater Paste,** fishing boat pictorial. £50-£75.
14. **Blanchflower Anchovy Paste,** barrel pictorial. £40-£50.
15. **Crosse & Blackwell's Anchovy Paste,** coat of arms. £12-£15.
16. **Crosse & Blackwell's Anchovy Paste,** unloading anchovies, brown print. £50-£75.
17. **Calverts Carbolic** t.p., 6d. £5-£10.
18. **Crapper & Brierley,** Hanley, Staffs., smiling lady. £250-£300.
19. **Cracrofts Areca nut** t.p., J. Pepper & Co., London. £5-£10.
20. **Creme D'Amande** Ambrosial, turreted tower t.m. £20+.

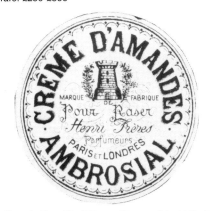

Above L. Type 20 - £20+ and R. one of the U.K's finest of building pictorials, referred to as the 'Bon Marche', type 10 - £250-£300.

147

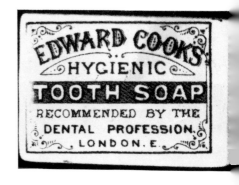

21. **Dr. Dosteels** pictorial of Queen Victoria, coloured background. £250-£300+.

22. **Edward Cooks,** rectangular lid. £15-£20.

23. **Ellen Hales, Mrs.,** celebrated heal-all ointment, lady pictorial. £30+.

24. **Gosnells,** Queen Victoria's side-on head, black & white. £10-£15.

25. **Gosnells,** Queen Victoria's side-on head, coloured. £15-£20.

26. **Hassalls, Dr.,** hair restorer, Farnworth, Manchester, bearded man, small. £50-£100.

27. **Icicles** pictorial, 'Cold Cream'. £7-£10.

28. **Jewsbury & Brown,** oriental t.p., Manchester, coat of arms pict., marbled border. £10-£15.

29. **Johnsons Celebrated Ointment,** Wrinehill, Nr. Crewe, pict. of house. £175-£200.

30. **Keddies** bloater paste or gorgona paste. £15-£20.

31. **Kranol Hair Food,** girl with long flowing locks. £75-£100+.

32. **Mannina Herbal Ointment,** Fishguard, several sizes; No. 1, no. 2 etc. £30+.

33. **Marbrero,** F.T. Leak, Harrogate, rect., pict. of tooth brush. £75-£100+.

34. **Otto of Rose Cold Cream,** stylized large vase of flowers. £20+.

35. **Ponds Areca Nut** t.p., small areca nut pict. £10+.

36. **Patrician** t.p. 'T. Churton & Co., Liverpool' , oval. £150-£200.

37. **Rookes Windsor Ointment,** Lincoln, bird on branch, small lid. £15-£20+.

38. **Russian Bears Grease,** bear with sash. £200+.

White Rose Tooth Paste.
1/6.

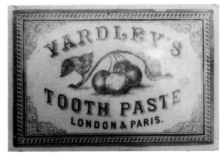

39. **Savages Celebrated Peruvian Balm,** overflowing vase of flowers, Guildford. £30-£50.

40. **Saunders Areca Nut** t.p., Liverpool, pict. of mosque & palm tree. £35-£50.

41. **Sharp Bros.,** cold cream, London. Harp in centre. £20-£30.

42. **Sharp Bros.,** as above but in red print. £30-£50.

43. **Trouchets Corn Cure,** small red printed lid featuring lighthouse. £15-£20+.

44. **Vinolia Shaving Soap,** London & New York, brown print. £20-£30.

45. **Woods,** 6d t.p., Plymouth, the worlds commonest pot lid? £5+.

46. **White Rose** t.p., S. Maw Son & Sons, London, square. £10+.

47. **Yardleys** t.p., London & Paris, coloured cherries, rect. £75-£100+.

Above, top L. type 39 - £30-£50, above R. type 40 - £35-£50. Centre L. type 45 - £5+, centre R. original ad' for type 46 - £10+. Directly above type 47 the Yardleys monochrome with coloured cherries and blue border, as with all overglaze decoration this is rarely completely intact which is why its price range is slightly broader, type 47 - £75-£100+.

MINI LIDS

Certain products required smaller containers – lip salves, eye ointment etc. Later domed lids, incorporating a much taller cylindrical glass base, also used smaller lids.

Top; display of lids all under 2 ins. diameter. Top R. type 26 - £50-£100. R. blue printed Lincoln dome-top, bottom L. similar dome-top from Boots. Bottom R. the very fine 'Wm. Burns'. All on this page are 1 1/2 to 2 ins. diameter.

Specialising in just one category of pot lids can help to marry together both rare and common items. Trevor King has a penchant for Anchovy Paste lids, as his award winning display above shows (Dorking 1984).

Right, the classic but common Burgess's type 11 - £5-£10, below L. type 15 - £12-£15, below R. type 30 - £15-£20.

Bears Grease pot lids have for a long while held an especial place in bottle collecting circles, the veritable hierarchial leaders? This is not difficult to understand why. Above' type 38 - £200+ shows evidence of its 100 years plus burial, but still a prized find in someones collection.

George Plummer, from Basingstoke, discovered this bears grease lid, incorporating a blue transfer, complete with contents and original paper label. £175-£200.

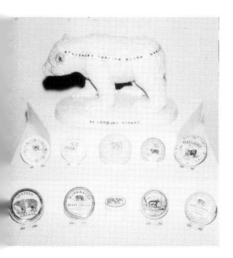

Above; a remarkable and significant display of bears grease lids, by Bert Latham, featuring as a backdrop an original pottery Atkinson's advertising window-display piece. The bottom row all have blue transfers!

Above R. and R. the 10/6d and £1/1/0d (guinea) size Atkinson's lids are both extremely rare.

Below L. highly detailed lid with a particularly decorative border. Below R. maybe the finest of 'em all – a brown printed lid from the Crown Perfumery Co.

Above, the £2,700 'Clayton & Cos Real Bears Grease, 58 Watling St., London' – that is the price it fetched at Sotheby's in November 1980. A highly detailed though macabre example.

R. a few years ago this circa 1870's lid was rated as "price by negotiation", however over a dozen examples surfaced from a Belfast dump in 1982, and a few more since. They are currently selling for £75-£100, though a place name or firm would make them considerably more collectable.

These reform flasks were reproduced in two tone stoneware by Baunes Pottery in the 1970's, one for each of the originals that they had previously made during the Reform period – £15-£20.

Henry Chesterman the well known Bristol bottle collector proudly displaying his large "Lord Broughan" Doulton flask over 14" high!! £400-£500.

Range of finely detailed and modelled Oldfield Pottery flasks (8" - 10") L. to R. "Sir Robert Peel" - £250-£300; "Old Tom" - £150-£200; "William IVth" - £250-£300; "Daniel O'Connell" - £300-£350.

REFORM FLASKS

These salt-glazed decorative flasks were produced during the period 1820 to 1856 and contained gin and probably other spirits.

They were produced at this time in large quantities all made by hand.

Lord Grey flask - inscribed "Grey Reform Cordial" "The True Spirit of Reform" - Doulton & Watts Pottery - £200-£250.

The main potteries that produced them were Joseph Bourne of Derbyshire; Doulton and Watts, Lambeth; Oldfield & Company, Chesterfield; Stephen Green, Lambeth; Frederick Wetherile, Lambeth; Woodhead, Davidson & Cooper of Bradford and Joseph Thompson, Woodville.

Some of these flasks are beautifully moulded with fine detail whilst others are very attractive because of their crudeness. The other main aesthetic quality they have are their subtle warm browns and buff colours whilst the "Oldfield" flasks are green/greys.

The subjects vary from the leading political figures of the day who were associated with the formulation of the Reform Act in 1832 to flasks commemorating royal and political figures together with historical events of that time.

The rarer flasks have dates, names of wine merchants or taverns, the sizes vary 3″ up to 15″ although the most common size is about 6½″/7″.

Opposite page:-

1. Flask of Victoria (9 1/4"). The moulding is copied from a portrait by Sir George Hayter - unmarked pottery. (3 different sizes). £200-£250.
2. Flask of "Lord John Russell" inscription "The True Spirit of Reform" - Doulton & Watts pottery. £150-£200.
3. "Queen Victoria 1st" Oldfield pottery. £250.
4. "Victoria" and "Albert" - unmarked pottery - (Note handles do not feature on pre-Victoria portrait flasks). £150-£200.
5. Figural flask of "Albert"- unmarked pottery (Similar flask with Brighton retailer marked). £250-£300+.
6. "Victoria" flask with "Duchess of Kent" on rear. Unmarked pottery. £150-£200.
7. "William IVth Reform Cordial" marked: "T Oldfield & Co. Manufacturers Chesterfield". £250-£300.
8. The opening of the Thames Tunnel flask unmarked pottery (1843). £800-£1,000.
9. Queen Victoria - on rear incised: "Queen Alexandrina Victoria" scroll on front "May Peace and Prosperity Prevail" - Bourne pottery. £150-£200.

photograph by courtesy of J. & J. May

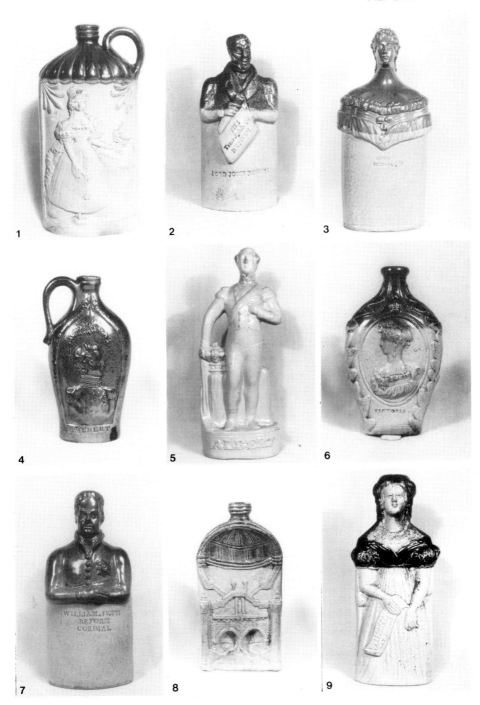

REFORM FLASKS

1 & 2: Pair of flasks marking the introduction of the Polka dance into Britain (c. 1844) - Pottery: Stiff Lambeth £500+.

3 & 4: A pair of rare unknown flasks - unmarked pottery. £250-£300+.

photograph by courtesy of J. & J. May

photograph by courtesy of J. & J. May

Above: Double-sided Flask of Queen Victoria on rear: Royal Coat of Arms (Note mistake in Coat of Arms: The use of the Hanoverian inescutcheon - this should have disappeared at the death of William IV - by Salic law no woman could hold the throne of Hanover. £250-£300+.Double-side flask of "Queen Victoria/ Duchess of Kent", in typcial dark brown "Nottingham" saltglazed - £120-£150.

REFORM FLASKS

REFORM FLASK SUBJECTS

1. Prince ALBERT
2. LADIES BOOT
3. Lord BROUGHAM
4. Queen CAROLINE
5. Mr. & Mrs. CAUNDLE
6. CLOCK Flask
7. COCKNEY man and woman
8. CRIMEAN WAR (end of!)
9. JIM CROW
10. FISH Flask
11. FOXES HEAD Stirrup Flask
12. Lord GREY
13. LADY with bird
14. MACE
15. MAN on Barrel
16. MAN with Peg-leg
17. LORD MELBOURNE
18. NAVVY off to the Crimean War
19. Daniel O'CONNEL M.P.
20. OLD QUEEN ELIZABETH'S HEAD (Tavern)
21. OLD TOM
22. Lord John RUSSELL

23. Sir Robert PEEL
24. Miss PETTYMAN
25. PISTOL Flask
26. POLKA (Man)
27. POLKA (Lady)
28. Mr. PUNCH
29. Mr. PUNCH ("The Triumph of the Pen")
30. SAILOR
31. SCEPTRE
32. THAMES TUNNEL
33. TOBACCO POUCH Flask
34. Queen VICTORIA
35. VICTORIA/ALBERT
36. VICTORIA/DUCHESS OF KENT
37. Duke of WELLINGTON
38. WILLIAM IVth
39. WORKMAN
40. Duke of YORK
41. TYNE TUNNEL
42. OLD WOMAN – KNARESBOROUGH
   (Mother Shipton)

These are portraits of (L. to R.): The Young Queen Victoria and The Duchess of Kent taken from a 'reform' jugs of this period see page 188.

Typical black glass free-blown onion wine bottle shape for the date. "Dated" examples of this period are extremely rare - £1,000-£2,000.

Sealed Bottles

The tradition of applying during manufacture of a small gob of molten glass on to a still malleable bottle which was then stamped with a customer's name or mark, town or village, began in the middle of the 17th century and is still seen on modern wine and spirt bottles of to-day. (They are of course moulded on to-day unless a special hand-blown bottle is made!)

Taverns and inns also had their own seals, as did many prominent people of the day. Later these seals were used by wine and spirit companies, commercial enterprises, colleges and glass manufacturers.

They appear on all shapes and types of bottles, flasks and jugs. One of the most sought after types are the 'dated' examples which were usually made to mark or commemorate some event of the day.

Facing page:–
Dates are approximate – the shapes evolved over varying periods with different glasshouses.

(1) c. 1630-1660 (shaft and globe).
(2) c. 1660-1670
(3) c. 1670-1680 (onion)
(4) c. 1680-1700 (onion)
(5) c. 1700-1715 (onion)
(6) c. 1715-1720 (onion)
(7) c. 1720-1730
(8) 1730-1750
(9) 1750-1760
(10) 1770-1780
(11) 1780-1800
(12) 1800-1820
(13) c. 1820–

From this date moulded bottles come into general use, first three piece moulds followed by two piece moulds, both with hand applied lips until c. 1920, when machine made bottles appeared.

Collections of sealed bottles are one of the few bottle 'types' to be found in Museums up and down the country.

These are mainly themes for 'sealed' bottle collectors to follow and prices vary from a sealed shaft and globe in four figures to a late Victorian vinegar or wine at a few pounds.

Two rare octagonal "sealed" bottles, L. to R.: Light green (rare colour) "C. E. 1734"; £1,500+; black glass "Manchester Infirmary" - a medical bottle.

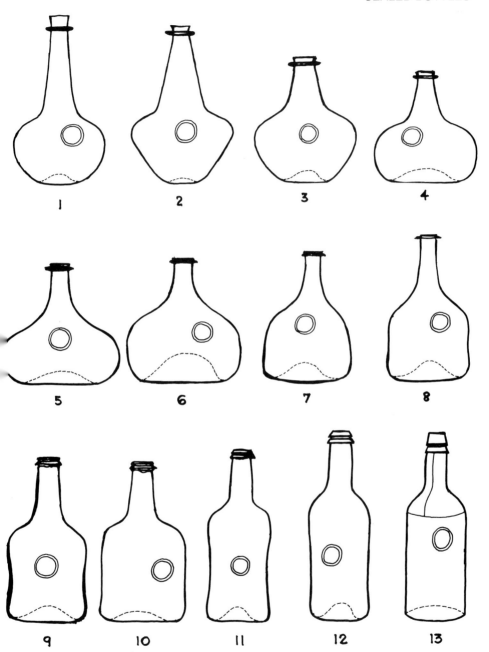

Development of the shape of the English wine bottle until the shape became silimar to that of modern bottles.

SEALED BOTTLES

Above: Black glass, sealed onion from the "Three Tuns" Tavern, Oxford (Licencees, Culpepper and Ann Tomlinson from 1695 to 1712) - £1,000.

Left: Short-neck free blown black glass, staff and globe wine bottle - £2,000. A similar bottle is listed in "sealed bottles" but: "T.L. 1687".

Group of free-blown black glass "sealed" wine bottles 1670-1720. Note the large magnum bottle, these are very rare for this period.

Typical French wine seal with date. Value of these types of sealed bottles – £5-£10.

Late nineteenth century sealed bottles.
Left to right: Black glass Dutch liqueur - £20+; German block, olive - £15-£20; black glass Dutch gin - £30-£50+;
Light green dated (see above) French wine - £5-£10.

Oval black glass moulded Irish spirit bottle (c. 1860 - 80) - £20-£30.

Extremely rare octagonal broken pontilled base Chemist's bottle, 8", (c. 1780-1800) - £300-£500+.

Typical English black glass sealed wine bottle of the period. This example is crude but with a large "crisp" seal. This "date" is very popular with the American Bottologists because it is the date of the "Independence" - £500+.

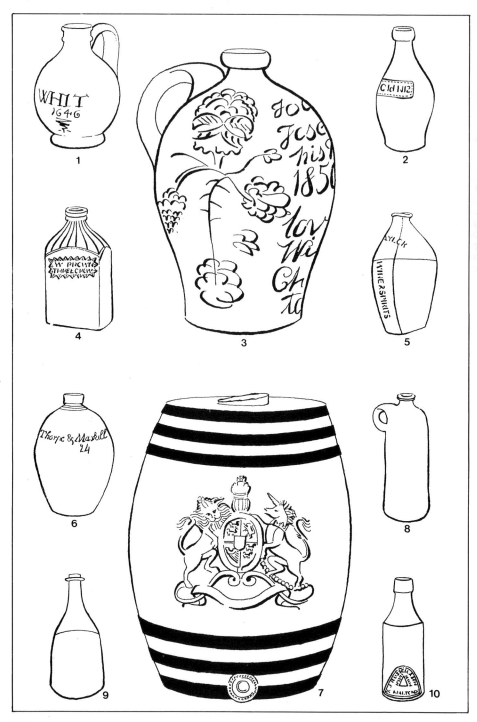

Stoneware

Very rare advertising tile 3″ x 3″ – sepia print on buff ground.

This is a broad title which roughly covers items before the widespread use of transfers. Early Victorian, and before, may give a clearer indication to what is envisaged as 'old stoneware', the majority of items included being salt-glazed. Due to the breadth covered in such a small space, it is hoped to sub-divide in the next book, and give greater emphasis to each category.

Facing page:-

1. Serving Bottle inscribed in blue: "Whit" "1646" (white wine), Delftware. £1,500-£2,000. (Beware of imitations).
2. Slab Seal spirit flask inscribed "Old No 12" (A Sheffield Inn), stoneware mid-19th century. £30-£50+.
3. Salt-glazed gin flask dated "1850" (country-style pottery) "Love to my Wife" etc. £300+.
4. Slab Seal spirit flask "W Brown": "Three Crowns", (c. 1840). £200+.
5. Pocket (hip) flask a London Wine Merchant's Stamp; Salt-glazed early 19th century. £50-£70.
6. Rare flagon "Thorpe and Maskill", "24", inscribed scraffito lettering, ash glaze, 18th century. (Possibly pharmaceutical). £100-£200.
7. Large salt-glazed barrel, "Doulton & Watts, Lambeth", early 19th century. £50-£100.
8. Salt-glazed bottle, German Mineral Water. £5-£10.
9. Stoneware Porter Bottle 2-tone, mid-19th century made by "Price, Bristol". £5+.
10. Late 19th dentury slip-glazed Yorkshire sealed bottle with triangular slab seal. £20-£30+.

Two-tone Scottish Whisky Flagon with applied decoration and royal coat of arms "James Dewar" (2 gallon size). £250-£300+.

We think these flagons were made to commemorate some anniversary or special event connected with certain companies.

STONEWARE

1. Snuff jar: Taddy and Co., buff glaze with black transfer. £50-£100.
2. Brown top G.B. "Cammack & Co.", "St. Helens". £15-£20
3. Brown salt-glazed Dutch gin bottle (c. 1800). £20+.
4. Scottish brown treacle glazed "Harvest" bottle (c. 1880). £50-£75.
5. Brown salt-glazed Bellarmine. £250-£400.
6. Blue lip G.B.: Clark & Co. Ltd. £150-£200+.
7. Cream pot - black transfer. £20-£30+.
8. Rare "churn" shaped China cream pot "By Royal Appointment". £30-£50.
9. Grey salt-glazed flask with applied lettered seal on side. £75-£100+.
10. Miniature two-tone stoneware whisk jug "Jorum". £50-£60.
11. Transfer printed food pot. £5-£10.
12. Miniature two-tone stoneware whisky jug "Auld Lang Syne" - "Sterling Whisky". £5+.

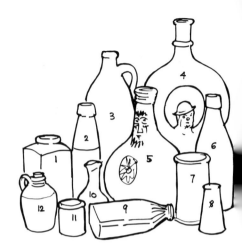

3 - two-tone salt-glazed cider/ale flagons, normally in two sizes, 1 gal. and 1/2 gal. L. to R.: John Barleycorn £150-£200; Souter Johnny £250-£300; John Barleycorn (different mould) - £150-£200; These do appear sometimes with Tavern or Landlord's names on, they are then £250-£300+.

Set of 3 1850/60's slab sealed ginger beers, L. to R.; 'William Carr, Blackburn' cart t.m.; 'John Claxton, Blackburn' cart-horse t.m.; Dated 'Coat of Arms' seal Blackburn '1859'.

STONEWARE

Bellarmines are probably the earliest items collected by bottlers. (Roman bottles holding little or no appeal in general).

Those with simply a face mask are the cheapest types, increasing in value as they diminish in size. Additional elaboration, body medals, etc., can have a sharp marked effect on raising the price too. Opposite a particularly desirable 1600 dated Bellarmine belonging to Bristol collector Henry Chesterman.

David Burton's superb display of Bellarmines shown at the Potteries Bottle Fayre in February 1980. The single most oustanding item of the Show was the early German Bellarmine, bottom left, which had recently been trawled up off the Sussex coast.

Diamond reg. on rear of bottle: 24th February, 1857.

Light brown treacle glazed tea-kettle ink incised -
"H. Morrel - London" - £50-£75.

Range of bottles colloquially referred to as Apollinaris. These vary in height and salt glaze colouring – from light orange through to dark brown. The front 3 are mid 19th century types, the larger R. hand piece is believed to be from the French 'Quimper' pottery of the late 18th century – rarely dug in the U.K.

Three two-tone salt-glazed druggists jars with applied Victorian coat of arms. The top ribbon seal incorporated gold leaf letting on a black background identifying the specific contents. L. to R. Cylindrical - £75-£100; Baluster shape - £75-£100+.

Salt-glazed stoneware beer flagon (1781-85) (8" high) - £50+.

A range of assorted stoneware on display stone of the early Burton-on-Trent Shows, Burton by Frank Burglin. The full range of 'stoneware' is covered here, slab seals, hip flasks, reforms, jugs, inks etc.

The range of grey/green slip glaze coloured slab seal pub flasks is now extremely extensive. The Nottingham/ Yorkshire/ Humberside/ Lincoln area have the greatest number available. L. to R.; - 'John Shaw/ Red Lion/ 44 White Friar Gate/ Hull' - £50-£75+; 'R. Irving/ Spirit Merchant/ Bakewell', rectangular cross section - £120-£150+. Scarce two-tone 'Sergeants & Co./ Brigg' - £100-£150.

A truly magnificent slab sealed veterinary bottle 'Gaskell's Celebrated Pleuro Pneumonia Medicine For Diseases Of Cows', and incorporating a cut-out cow shape slab below. Only one example recorded. £500+.

Veterinary

By Royal Warrant to
H.M. The King.

By Royal Warrant to
H.M. The King.

DAY & SONS, ESTABLISHED 1840.
CREWE. LTD (CREWE)
HORSE, CATTLE, SHEEP & DOG MEDICINES.

The Veterinary trade progressed at a similar rate to the Quack Doctors/Medics. However, farmers generally were more loath to accept veterinary bills and doubted the skills or curative powers of any of the new fangled medicines. In most instances the 'vet' was called in too late to offer assistance and his consequent failure further perpetuated doubts amongst the 'old guard'.

Progress was gradually made though, and there arose a necessity for pre-packed products, available off the shelf. Sales increased dramatically from then on, creating a massive influx of new products for animals of all kinds.

Few bottle collectors have really researched this intriguing area to any depth. Steve Day from London has, not too surprisingly, researched into the histories of 'Day & Sons, Crewe' & 'Day Son & Hewitts, London' (two firms who are often mistakenly connected).

Most farms have a dormant dump on their land, possibly suggesting the future scope within this category? The pottery products prove to be especially appealing to present day collectors.

DAYS' BLACK DRINK

Cures Colic or Gripes in Horses or Cattle, Scour and Weakness in all Young Stock, Blown Cattle and Sheep, Debility, Chills, and Low Condition in all Stock.

Price 1/8 per bottle.

DAYS' HUSKOLEIN.

Almost infallible for Tape Worms in Lambs and other Animals; for Husk or Hoose in Calves, Lambs, &c. A speciality for Worms in Horses and Colts.

6/6 per bottle.

DAY & SONS' "ORIGINAL" MEDICINE CHESTS

L.; original advertising for the products from 'Day & Sons, Crewe', a town situated in the heart of the rich Cheshire farmlands. They manufactured a wide range of products, with bottles varying from dense green and having cork tops, through to clear examples having external screw caps, but nevertheless interesting if complete with original labels.

ESSENTIALS TO EVERY FARM & STABLE.

177

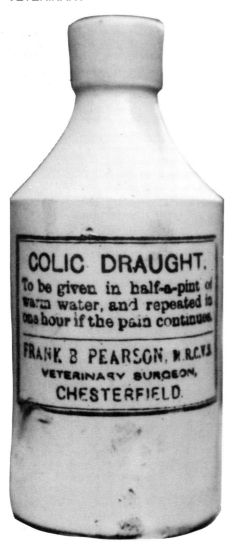

VETERINARY

1. Day & Sons, Gaseous Fluid, Crewe. Small aqua bottle, square section. £1.
2. Day & Sons, Gaseous Fluid, Crewe. Deep green bottle, square section. £5-£10.
3. Day & Sons Red Drink, or Black Drink. Labelled, square section, screw top. £3-£5.
4. Day Son & Hewitts Chemical Extract, London. Square with facetted corners, cobalt. £20-£30.
5. Colic Draught, Frank B. Pearson, M.R.C.V.S., Veterinary Surgeon, Chesterfield. Rare transferred pot, bulk-ink shape. £10-£20.
6. Gaskells Celebrated Pleuro Pneumonia Medicine For Diseases of Cows. A stunning pictorial slab seal, rect. shape. £500+.
7. Thorleys Poultry Spice, cylindrical pot with pigs head t.m. on one side. £100+.
8. Thorleys Food, Vitum Powder For Horses, transferred advertising ash tray. £40-£50+.

Above; rare transferred stoneware bottle, similarly shaped to bulk-inks, except just 5 ins. tall. A number of regional variations on this theme – colic drench, colic draught etc. For future volumes we would appreciate further types/listings?

HARVEY'S
Worm & Condition Powders

(May be Sold Retail by Chemists only)

Are used in all Leading Studs, and are pronounced by Mr. W. GUY STEVENS, the famous Trainer, to be **"The Best Worm Powders for Horses in existence."**

Horses using them require no Rest from Work or alteration in Feeding.

PRICES: Box of 15 Powders, **3/-**; or with Patent Physic Ball, **3/9.**

Above; A range of impressively transferred items from 'Thorleys'. Top; both sides of a cylinder, not dis-similar from cream pot types, for 'Thorleys Poultry Spice'. Bottom; a Thorleys advertising ash tray featuring what looks like a very elaborate tin in the centre?

WATER FILTERS

Prior to our fluoride-flavoured tap water, direct from reservoir and pumping station, the nation relied upon unsanitary plumbing and unclean wells, even stream water.

Various devices were employed, with varying degrees of success, to filter the water. The mid Victorian to late Edwardian solution – pottery filters varying in size up to 10 gallons capacity, have survived remarkably ove the last 100 years or more.

Their styles are as varied as their sizes; plain cream/ off-white examples with applied slab-sealed-type decorations, salt glaze waisted ones, transferred cylindrical shapes, and the truly up-market, colourful, and decorative, Doulton artwares, often standing on elegant pedestals.

Though mostly large they lend themselves to other uses today – holding potted plants, doubling up as a trendy umbrella stand, whilst the smaller ones can be easily incorporated in a broad display of bottles. The coloured Doulton ones look just right on the sideboard, where they were originally designed for.

This filter now nestles in New Zeland and attractively houses a large plant in a collecots' garden. 'The Cheavin Microbe Proof Filter, Manufactured By The Fulham Pottery & Cheavin Filter Co. Ltd., London, S.W.', certainly a long way from home? £30+ without lid.

Two fairly large filters, both with their original lids. L. elaborate Doulton-made example with Royal Coat of Arms amidst all the swirls. R. 'W. M. Jowett & Co., Manchester' with numerous applied slabs, one showing George & the Dragon. Cream body, slabs in white with lettering picked out in black. Complete examples £100-£150+.

Advertisement for J. H. Graham Filters. The one in centre is described as "... drab stoneware and white decoration" also sold "... for ship use encased in wicker"!

WATER FILTERS

1. Small off-white filter with applied slab seal decoration. Fairly mundane. £30-£50.
2. Waisted types, such as Lipscombe & Cos., dark brown salt glaze. £75-£100.
3. As previous but lighter saltglaze and straight sided lower portion, normally these are Doulton made. £75-£100.
4. As 2 & 3 but body cream, white slab seals, sometimes parts picked out in black. These are normally from Lipscombes. £50-£75.
5. Tall straight sided. Off-white body with applied white plaques and much of the lettering picked out in black. £30-£50.

6. Tall straight sided cylindrical shape incorporating elaborate transfer, such as 'Doultons Manganous Carbon Filter' or 'The Cheavin Microbe Proof Filter'. £100-£150+.
7. Coloured Doulton artwares, with raised decoration. Often on elegant pedestal. More often than not seen at Antique auctions. £200-£500.
8. Doulton coloured miniature 'samples' Approx. 4 ins. £500-£750+.

All of the above are approx. prices according to desirability, amount of decoration etc. The inside 'bits', lids, original taps etc. do not necessarily effec the price.

Two highly distinctive Doulton made pedestal artware filters, obviously manufactured for the 'posher' homes!

WATER JUGS

Ceramic and glass jugs are collected in a wide variety of categories from the early salt-glazed items of the early 1800's up to the modern day 'Pub-Jugs'. They vary in price from four figures to a couple of pounds for the modern variety which presents collectors with a very wide scope.

Samples of most of the jugs covered in these volumes do appear in Victorian and later dumps. Some very interesting broken pieces have also come from earlier dumps sometimes 'unknown' as whole items as is also the case with pot-lids etc.

They can advertise anything from early pottery manufacturers through all types of commercial firms – 'Hatters', 'Grocers', shops etc., to the most common which were for ales, beers, spirits, mineral waters and laterly cigarettes etc.

They were made by nearly all the famous potteries connected with the manufacture of ceramic bottles etc.. The glass types are much rarer and were only produced in relatively small quantities.

Apart from the early types they all turn up at most Antique and Flea-markets and even cheap damaged examples can display well.

During the last 20 years "pub-jugs" have been very popular with all the major breweries, distilleries and cigarette manufacturers as a form of advertising and have been produced in large quantities. These are readily available and turn up at most bottle shows for a few pounds each.

"Fred Archer" jug commemorating the Derby winner of 1857 - £150-£200+.

photograph by courtesy of "Pub-Jugs & other Advertising Jugs"

Two-tone salt-glazed Doulton whisky jug "Thomas Cunningham & Sons", "Excalibur, Scotch and Irish Whiskey" - £250-£300+.

Three contrasting Pub-jugs. L. to R.: "Greyhound", "Green Label Scotch": - green mottle with black print - £80-£120; Royal Doulton, Kingsware, "Memories" with Charles Dickens as the central portrait surrounded by his characters - £50-£75; "Black and White Scotch", black print - £30-£40+.

Below, water jug advertising a tailor "G. W. Villar" - £200+.

Above:- A set of very rare two-tone, saltglazed jugs advertising "James Stiff and Sons, Lambeth Pottery, London" - £200-£300.

Left: - An interesting water jug advertising the "Pomona Hotel," "H.E. Haycock" - £100-£150.

Green top, "Eadie's". "Gleneagles", "Fine Old Scotch" - £75-£100; Brown top, "Dandy Dinmont Scotch Whisky" - £125-£150+.

Three Doulton items. Left: Green topped John Dewars & Son, £80-£100+ - also available without the frontal transfer, £50-£75. Rare Doulton Belarmine style, £75+. Colourful Victoria Jubilee commemorative jug, in blue, greens and browns, £100+.

A collection of stoneware "Pub-Jugs" showing variety of shapes, designs and sizes, the back three probably used for pouring out ale - freshly drawn from the cellar barrels - the front ones used for water, to add to whisky. L. to R: Kings Head Aylesbury £40+; all tan William & Neal Bucks £75-£100; W. Forsyth, Oldham £30+; unusual decorative tall china jug W. C. Townsend Free Beer Stores Penistone, £100-£150; early impressed Wrexham jug £50-£75; blue top, blue transfer Ruthin (N. Wales) beer jug £100-£150; small 'Plough Inn' Wenlock Edge £40-£50+.

WATER JUGS

Two-tone, salt-glazed water jug - "Soames" "Welsh Ale" - £60-£80.

The most impressive and rare ("one off") saltglazed water jug - advertising "J. Champions XX Ale" (15" high) also in applied decoration is "Carrington", "The Royal Coat of Arms", "The Young Queen Victoria", "The Duchess of Kent" together with beautifully sculptured rural drinking scenes - £50-£75+. (We think this must be the "Grandaddy" of all pub-jugs!!). It is also dated "1839" - £500-£750.

photograph by courtesy of "Pub-Jugs and other Advertising Jugs"

"AND HERE'S A HAND, MY TRUSTY FRIEN,
AND GIE'S A HAND O' THINE,
AND WE'LL TAK A RIGHT GUID WILIE WAUGHT,
FOR AULD LANG SYNE."

REGISTERED

Above; the Auld Lang Syne whisky features one of the most highly detailed transfers, as well as incorporating a diamond registration mark (by the feet). Fortunately it is one of the most available jugs for collectors and it is quite reasonably priced. Type 1, £60-£100.

Whisky Crocks

In England we refer to them as whisky jugs, some Australians refer to them as whisky crocks, but everyone knows that highly elaborately transferred whisky containers are what is meant. Further glowing examples of the Victorian engravers art.

They have tremendous associations with the gold-rush days in Scotland, Wales, but most especially Australia. The heavy drinkers of the shanty mining towns, the rough and ready miners, where the living was hard, can easily be imagined swigging out of the relatively strong pottery receptacles.

The range is very extensive, and new varieties continue to appear, especially during the last 3 years when English collectors have become far keener on them.

Above; L. Carnegie Brae, Aberdeen, type 4, £50-£75. R. Long John's Dew of Ben Nevis, Fort William, type 15, £120-£150.

A fair amount of Glengelts, type 10, survived because they were often encased in a protective leather coat. Usually sold for £60-£75+.

L. a rare Lincolnshire jug, type 13, £80-£100+ (about 5 known). R. large Barley Brae, type 2, £80-£100+.

L. Heather Dew, The Greybeard, a relatively common pictorial, type 11, £30-£50. R. blue transferred 'Dublin Pot Still, New York', type 8, £100+.

Variations on the Masons mallet shape. L. t.t. with slab sealed masonic symbols, type 16, £100-£200. R. a rare 'Perfection, J.J. McCallum, type 17, £50-£75+.

Above; L. Glen Garry, featuring a corkscrew, type 9, £40-£50. R. bulk two gallon flagon 'John Dewars', type 7, £75-£100.

1. Auld Lang Syne. Highly ornate transfer of 3 seated men drinking at tavern table, all surrounded by garland of thistles, verse at top. Also incorporates diamond registry mark in black transfer. Neck tan. £60-£100.

2. Barley Brae. Some similarity to type 1, though background less busy. Three men seated drinking at table. Tan neck. £80-£100+.

3. Buchanan, James, House of Commons. One of the most sought after whiskies, tan neck, highly detailed sepia transfer of Houses of Parliament and busy street scene in front. £400-£500.

4. Carnegie Brae, Aberdeen, Finest Scotch Malt. Overall pear shape with a flattened base. Two sizes available, both with tan neck. £50-£75.

5. Cruiskeen Lawn, Mitchell's, Belfast. Tan neck. One of the commonest whiskies but the highly elaborate black transfer, scrolls etc., makes it appealing. £40-£50.

6. Dawson's Perfection, Dufftown, Glenlivet District. Long dark brown neck with pouring lip. Sepia transfer. £120-£150+.

7. Dewar, John. Large t.t. flagon, 2 galls. Transfer on shoulder imitating a label. Quite rare. £75-£100.

8. Dublin Pot Still, New York. Brown neck. Blue transfer. All lettering surrounded by leaves. £100+.

9. Glen Garry, Very Old Scotch Whisky, John Hopkins & Co. Tan neck with pouring lip. Transfer features a corkscrew. £40-£50.

10. Glengelt, Wm Stenhouse & Co., Glasgow. Tan neck. Small rampant lion in centre. £60-£75+.

11. Heather Dew, Greybeard, Mitchell Bros., Glasgow. Straight sided, stumpy brown neck. Transfer features 2 kilted Scotsmen toasting one another. Quite common. £30-£50.

12. Jeroboam, Stag Blend. Brown neck. Small stag pictorial with leaves and branches going right round body. Fairly common. £30-£50.

13. Johnson, Basker & Fletcher, Grantham. Rare Lincolnshire whisky. Brown neck, lettering surrounded by thistles etc. £80-£100.

14. Kingsware, Doulton. This extensive range is most varied, featuring slip-coloured figures on a shiny dark brown background. Some of the pieces are extremely rare and rising rapidly in value. Generally prices are £100-£1,000+.

15. Long John's, Dew of Ben Nevis. Brown neck. Hand holding cross, all surrounded by foliage. Three different sizes. £120-£150.

16. Masonic Mallet, dark brown bulbous neck, cream body covered in applied masonic symbols. £100-£200.

17. Perfection, J. J. McCallum, Edinburgh, Glasgow & London. Mallet shape with brown neck, black transfer. £50-£75+.

Two jugs with sepia transfers. L. 'James Buchanan, House of Commons', type 3, £400-£500, with detailed crowd in front and many horse drawn wagons. R. 'Dawson's Perfection' Glenlivet District, type 6, £120-£150+.

Above; Kingsware 'Britannia' flask, manufactured for Dewars, with a very brightly coloured picture. Not strictly Kingsware, but accepted amongst this most extensive range. All are Doulton made, most have a predominantly dark brown background. £200-£250+.

Right; An extremely rare multi-coloured 'Golfers' Kingsware jug. Instead of the more usual brown background this has bright colours - yellow, light blue etc., £1,000+, brown version £400-£500.

Rare light grey "Mallet" stoneware whisky crock with sepia print - £200-£250.

THE ILLUSTRATED LONDON NEWS, JULY 10, 1897.—59

"IN GENERAL USE."

A Commanding Spirit finds its way to the front. PATTISONS' WHISKY commands success because it has been found by the public to be a genuine, wholesome, palatable beverage, carefully blended and thoroughly matured. It is cream-like in taste, with all the stimulating qualities of the pure Highland spirit. Sold Here, There, and Everywhere.

Sole Proprietors: **PATTISONS, Ltd.,** Highland Distillers, **BALLINDALLOCH, LEITH, AND LONDON.**

Much sought after "Sunderland, Grant, Mackey & Co." this is the large version with a royal blue body (12" high) - £1,000-£1,500.

Bibliography

Pot Lids
The t.p. Pot Lid Booklet. Ben Swanson. Private pub.
The Price Guide to b & w pot lids. Ronald Dale. A.C.C.
B & w pot lids by Jane Heath. Salter Collect. Publications
The Advertising Art of Painted Pot Lids by R. Green & D. Lewis. O.B. & TH.
Collecting Pot Lids – coloured b & w with prices by A. Ball. M.A.B. Pub.
Price Guide to Pot Lids (coloured) by A. Ball. A.A.C.
Collecting Pot Lids, Fletcher. Pitman 1975

Cream Pots
Collecting Cream Pots by Chris Hunt. Private pub.
Dairy Cream Pots by Chris Hunt. Private pub.

Clay Pipes
Prospecting & Collecting Clay Pipes by John Webb & Alex Childs 1976
Clay Pipes by E. Fletcher. S. C. Pub. 1977.
Clay Tobacco Pipes by Eric Gayton. Shire Albums 1979.

Mineral Waters
Aerated Water Machinery by Will Chester. Master.
Marble Bottles by Edward Fletcher.
Mainly Codds Wallop by R. Morgan 1974.
Mineral Water Bottles by B. Wynn-Jones. Salter Collect Pub. 1978.

Inks
The Collectors Book of Ink Bottles by June Tansley. Private pub. 1976.
The Collectors 3rd Book of Ink Bottles by June Tansley. Private pub. 1977.
The Collectors Book of Ink Bottles by J. Tansley, editor A. Payne. S. c. Pub. 1980.
Ink Bottles & Inkwells by W. E. Covill.

Seals/black glass
Sealed Bottles their history and era. 1630-1930 by R. Morgan. Midlands M.A.B. Pub. 1980.
Sealed Bottles their history & evolution 1630-1930 by R. Morgan. Sutton Coll. Pub. 1980
Nailsea Glass by Keith Vincent. David & Charles 1975.

Ginger Beers
Ginger Beer Collectors Manual by E. Fletcher. B & R Pubs. 1974.
Ginger Beer Collecting, Adams, Payne & Davison. S. Coll. Pubs. 1976.
Norfolk Ginger Beer Bottles by T. Davy & D. Clairfield. Private pub. 1977.
Collecting Ginger Beers & Stouts by J. England & M. Bithell. Private pub. 1981.

Stoneware/Pottery
Stoneware Bottles, 1500-1949 by D. Ashey. Brown Graphics 1981.
English Brown Stoneware, 1670-1900 by Oswald, Hildyard & Hughes. Faber & Faber 1982.
Browne Muggs – English Brown Stoneware by R. Hildyard. V & A 1985.
English & Scottish Earthenware by G. Bernard Hughes. Abbey Fine Arts.
Statues that Pour by Otta D. Wearin. U.S.A. 1965.
A Collectors Guide to Olde Whisky Jugs by Les Martin. Private pub. 1977.
Jugs, A Collectors Guide by James Paton. Souvenir Press 1976.

General
English Glass Bottles by Geoffrey Wills. John Bartholomew & Son 1974.
Antique Bottles in Colour by E. Fletcher. Blandford Press 1976.
Bottles & Bygroves by Eileen & Al Lastovica. Cape Town 1982.
A Treasury of Bristol Bottles by R. Green. OB. & TH. 1982.
Digging up Antiques by E. Fletcher. Pitman Publishing 1975.

Price Guides
British Bottle Collectors Price Guide by A. Blakeman & M. Smith. B.B.R. 1983.
Antique Glass Bottles by G. Litherland. M.A.B. Pub. 1975.
The Bristol Bottle Price Guide by T. Reynolds & G. Litherland. M.A.B. 1975.
Bottle Collecting Price Guide by R. Green. OB & TH. 1977.

Quacks/Medicine
Collecting All Cures by Bill Agee. Fexion Press 1973.
Poison Bottles, Collectors Guide, by R. Durflinger. Maverick 1975.
Collecting Quack Cures by A. McEwan. Private pub.
The Benigh Blue Coffin (Poisons) by R. Morgan. Kollectorama Pub. 1978.
Great Armenian Pontilled Medicines by Frederick Nielsen. Private Pub. 1978.
Antiques of the Pharmacy by L. Matthews. W & J Mackey 1971.

Doulton related items
The Doulton Story by Paul Atterbury & Louise Irvine. Doulton Books 1979.
Doulton Burslem Advertising Wares by Jocelyn Lukins, published by Venta Books.
Doulton Kingsware Whisky Flasks by Jocelyn Lukins, published by Venta Books.